Praise for

"Tina, along with her mother Millie and sister Susan, received the National Council for Community Behavioral Healthcare's 2006 Award for Excellence in Consumer and Family Support. The award honors those who use their personal experiences to help others struggling to live with and recover from mental illness. In this book, Tina shares her family's story, providing hope not only to individuals experiencing a mental illness, but to all those who love and support them. It is a powerful story that's as inspirational as it is moving."

Linda Rosenberg, MSW, CSW
President & CEO
National Council for Community Behavioral Healthcare

"*Saving Millie: A Daughter's Story of Surviving Her Mother's Schizophrenia* by Tina Kotulski is a compelling and poignant narrative based on the author's true life experiences as she attempts to maneuver through the quagmire of her mother's undiagnosed mental illness and the inadequacies of our mental health care system.

Saving Millie adeptly demonstrates the necessity for research to ensure early and accurate diagnosis and appropriate treatments for the successful management of schizophrenia, as well as the importance of providing education, support services and information to family members whose lives are so personally affected by this overwhelming and devastating illness.

Saving Millie is a story about hope, courage and love and is helpful in illustrating the facts surrounding the illness of schizophrenia which is so often misunderstood. Thank you to Tina Kotulski for sharing her story and giving the illness of schizophrenia not only a face, but a family."

Olimpia Etts, Student
School of Social Welfare at Stony Brook University

Saving Millie

Saving Millie

A daughter's story of surviving her mother's schizophrenia

Tina Kotulski

Extraordinary Voices Press, LLC

Saving Millie: A Daughter's Story of Surviving Her Mother's Schizophrenia

The names of some nonfamily members used in this book have been changed. Photos and letters are taken from the author's private collection. All quotes from interviews conducted by Susan Smiley are used with permission. The letter excerpt appearing on page 194 is used with permission from David Rose.

Extraordinary Voices Press, LLC
P.O. Box 164
Madelia, MN 56062

www.extraordinaryvoices.com

ISBN: 0-9779115-1-9
ISBN-13: 978-0-9779115-1-6

Cover Design: George Foster, www.fostercovers.com
Interior Design & Typesetting: Liz Tufte, www.folio-bookworks.com
Printed in the U.S.A.

Dedication

For those who have grown up in the shadow of mental illness.

Contents

Foreword

For many years, the families of those diagnosed with schizophrenia were truly invisible victims of the disease. Not only the *de facto* caregivers of first and last resort, always on duty to avert crises and pick up pieces, family members were also regarded as the very cause of their loved ones' suffering. Elaborate theories detailed the personality types and family dynamics that, it was said, gave rise to schizophrenia and other serious mental illnesses.

Fortunately, the scientific revolution in psychiatry has dramatically increased our understanding of the etiology of schizophrenia. While stressful social environments do seem to play some role in the development of the disease, genetics and neurobiology appear to be much more significant—indeed, usually decisive—factors.

Rather than blame and guilt, families need substantial help in dealing with the pain, frustration, and exhaustion of living with mentally ill family members. Mental health professionals have, in recent years, developed new and effective techniques to aid families enduring this ordeal. Even more importantly, families and friends have banded together to provide mutual encouragement and assistance. Unfortunately, these positive changes have come slowly, and all too many families remain alone with their struggles.

Saving Millie: A Daughter's Story of Surviving Her Mother's Schizophrenia is a much-needed contribution to this effort to foster awareness about mental illness and support for families who live with it. Tina Kotulski's poignant account of her experience turns a powerful light on the impact mental illness has on families, particularly on the children of afflicted parents. Tina's story will no doubt resonate with—and give hope to—many people who struggle to cope in similar circumstances. *Saving Millie* also presents a sobering and thorough picture of the family experience of mental illness that professionals must fully comprehend in order to better serve both their patients and the people who love them.

Marvin Swartz, M.D.
Professor and Head
Division of Social and Community Psychiatry
Department of Psychiatry and Behavioral Sciences
Duke University Medical Center
Durham, North Carolina

Acknowledgements

MY DEEPEST THANKS GO TO THE FOLLOWING:

To God, for helping me to find peace and security and making me realize that my strength and confidence can only come from within.

To my child psychiatrist, Dr. Klapman, and to all the therapists at Old Orchard Hospital who refused to give up on me—even when I was ready to give up on myself.

To Julie and Richard Greene, Lynda Bendik, Ray and Mary McClellan, and Jeffrey Kotulski, D.O., for their belief, compassion and proficient editorial skills that made this project all the more powerful.

To Michael Borum of etherweave communications, for his excellent design work and building of my web site —
www.extraordinaryvoices.com

To George Foster, whose sophistication and ability to convey the meaning behind this story made for a beautiful cover design.

To Liz Tufte, whose meticulous layout and interior design gave beauty to these words.

To Sharon Castlen, for getting this book out there.

To Lynda Bendik for her thorough typing and proofreading comments on a draft version of the manuscript.

To the Daughters and Sons of Parents with Mental Illness panel members with whom I had the pleasure serve: Joe Donovan, Maggie Jarry, Heather Burack, M.S.W.; Chia Ying Wei; Mary Ann Widenhouse; Kate Biebel, Ph.D.; Lucinda Sloan-Mallen; Dr. Anand Pandya; and Jim McNulty. You so courageously shared your memories, experiences, and insights; you helped me see the importance of this story.

To all the friends, family members, and professionals who read one of the early drafts and were honest and caring enough to share a bit of themselves: John Hall; Nancy Eckstrom; Larry and Brenda Smiley; Susan Smiley; Barb Letarte; Lynda Bendik; Doris Osborne; Dr. Stephen M. Goldfinger; Julie and Richard Greene; Ray and Mary McClellan; Katie Zaman; Judge Allison L. Krehbiel; Dr. Jim and Katie Eiselt; Missy Stolt; Tana Lunz; Stacie Gerhardt; Peggy Olson; Audrey Knewtson; MaryJo Halverson; Barb and Willard Reed; Michelle Van Hee; Kristen Kienholtz; Jay Neugeboren; David W. Koehser, J.D.; Olimpia Etts; Xavier Amador, Ph.D.; and Dr. Marvin Swartz.

To my mother Millie, for always doing the best she could and for never giving up.

Finally, to my husband Jeff, for being my angel through all this, and to our three children: You complete me.

Faith is the patient seamstress
Who mends our torn belief,
Who sews the hem of childhood trust
And clips the threads of grief.

– Joan Walsh Anglund
Author of *A Cup of Sun*

Beneath the Surface of Our Lives

Very late on school nights, my mother Millie would take my sister and me to Jewel-Osco, the local grocery store. Often, we went because our mother just wanted to get out of the house. While she stood in front of the mirror and applied makeup—some blush and a coat of lipstick—Susan and I hurried to arrange ourselves at the door. Our mother, dressed in jeans, wore her long auburn hair in a loose chignon, her lips the color of ripe peaches.

She was beautiful, willowy, ethereal—like a sister of Grace Kelly. With high, prominent cheekbones and big brown eyes, our mother often looked out at the world as if she were flirting with it and, at the same time, resisting it. Her beauty could cast an aura, one in which men lingered. Women simply turned away, as if they might lose something in her presence.

But Millie was oblivious of all of this. In her mind, she was simply ordinary. Many times, I'd stand at her side while she spread on lipstick and fussed with her hair. I wanted to tell her how pretty she was—that she was the prettiest of all the mothers I knew—but somehow I couldn't, and she remained unaware of my adoration. She'd pile her hair on top of her head, fastening it with bobby pins.

Frustrated for no apparent reason, she'd yank out the pins, letting her hair fall back down. Then she'd grab a tissue, and off came the lipstick. I'd watch as she'd become exasperated, wondering what she saw in the mirror that made her feel so unattractive. It had to be something only she could see.

When I was a bit older, I dedicated myself to bolstering her self-esteem. I wanted only one thing: to make my mother feel good about herself. "Everything's just flat on me," she'd say with disgust, complaining about her breasts and bottom. One year, I saved enough money babysitting to buy her padded underwear, which gave the illusion of a rounded bottom. I gave them to her for Christmas, but she only looked at me blankly, slightly offended, and wouldn't even try it on; it took her a while to see that my intentions were good. Later, she laughed about it but still had my grandmother dutifully pack up my present and send it back.

Some nights, we were the only ones in the store. Closing time was midnight, and we'd often have to rush a bit beneath the glare of the man at the checkout counter. The three of us would shop swiftly, silently. Our mother would go to the vitamin aisle first, lingering there while my sister and I reviewed the costume jewelry, arguing when we picked out the same piece. Then, if there was time, we picked up fresh chicken, milk, eggs, ingredients to make fudge, and TV dinners.

The periods when our mother's rage would subside were rare, yet they remain vivid to me. When she was calm, we savored her laughter, her jokes, and the relief from the tension that haunted our daily lives.

During these fleeting moments, our mother was far different from the woman who'd often sit, day after day, watching TV (usually a Cubs game or late-night static), staring off into the distance and chain-smoking. At those times, the curtains would be drawn in the living room, and she'd sit cross-legged, swinging one leg, mumbling, perhaps brooding about past heartaches.

It was never clear to us what caused her emotions to shift so suddenly—the postman, our neighbors, the ring of the telephone, her fear that my sister and I were talking behind her back. Nor, for that matter, did we know what made our mother happy. We became silent prisoners to her mercurial moods, mincing around as if on eggshells, speaking in hushed tones. Even when I was five and Susan seven, our behavior was nuanced and painfully accommodating.

For many years, I believed that I could manage my mother's emotions and complex moods—even predict them like the phases of the moon. But Susan didn't have such confidence or aspirations; she chose, instead, to steer clear of the great waves of feeling that washed over our mother. I dug in my heels, insisting, if only to myself, that I was the sole reason for our mother's emotional vicissitudes.

I would tell her jokes:

Cow much do I love you?

Watch, Mom, I can *fry* like an eagle!

And she would be genuinely amused. "Oh, *Tina*," she'd say, waving me off, "you are something."

She had a laugh that could alter the mood of an entire room. I wanted to keep her happy, not only for her sake but also for mine. I'd dance, put on shows, dash in and out of the house as fast as I could—anything to ward off the darkness. When I ran out of jokes or my performances didn't produce the desired effect, I sank, feeling the way I thought my mother must have felt: helpless and unloved.

Eventually, I became especially talented at intercepting things that seemed to affect my mother's emotional state adversely. The telephone, for example, had its own way of setting her off. At best, it was an interruption for her; at worst, it was part of a conspiratorial scheme to rob us of our privacy, to confiscate our innermost thoughts and secrets. If Susan or I did pick up the telephone, which our mother often forbade us to do, she would scream at us. "Hang up!" she'd insist, terrified. "Hang up now!" Sometimes it was our grandmother calling to check on us, and other times a crank call. Yet, either scenario created for her—and for us—the same level of threat.

When we left the Jewel-Osco with our bags of groceries, it was often near midnight. At home, we'd unpack in a hurry. Then, while we heated up our TV dinners, Millie would hover over the stove, making fudge, something we ate nearly every night.

Often, the summer months seemed to sustain her good phases, as if strong sunlight could pierce her personal darkness. Millie would sit outside in the morning in her yellow bikini, her hair pulled back, a sheen of baby oil along her shoulders and legs. She'd spend long afternoons sunning in our back yard. Susan and I would seize the opportunity to take off on our bikes. Susan would go one way, I another. During those rare afternoons, we were just kids with a mother at home sunning herself, all of us just like everyone else.

In the summer, our neighborhood was ripe for adventure; long, lush green days encouraged us to throw off our dreary winter routines. In the evenings, there were barbecues, softball games, and an annual carnival. The local swimming pool, which we usually joined, teemed with kids and mothers who seemed friendlier than usual.

For me, those long bike rides were more of an emotional break than anything else. I never dreamed of permanently escaping, as I imagine Susan might have. She'd ride outside of town, but I stayed within the bounds of our neighborhood, remaining beneath the canopy of old elms that lined the streets, never quite reaching the safe, normal place where I thought everyone else around us dwelt.

Instead, I derived pleasure from danger, seeing how close I could get to the edge. I rode on streets, as fast as cars, zipping through stop signs. I ignored the rules of the road and tried to outmaneuver traffic. I'd do it in front of police officers, taunting them. Sometimes, a policeman on bike patrol would stop me and hand me a warning slip. I collected these slips and used them, brazenly, to wallpaper one corner of my room. That seemed to charm my mother—something I interpreted as pride.

If I weren't on my bike, I could be found jumping from the garage roof or scaling tree branches. Often, I'd play in the back yard, which was always a bit unkempt—long wild grass and overgrown bushes bordering our neighbors' properties prevented anyone from seeing in—the way our mother liked it. Sometimes, on windy days, strange sounds came from the bushes and frightened me. I imagined someone living in there, waiting for just the right moment to jump out and snatch me. In some ways, I think I was hoping for this.

After a particularly sweltering summer day, the three of us would sometimes sip lemonade together, listening to the chorus of cicadas that made their appearance at night. Like a rare alignment of the planets, we sat there, all with the same wish: to wait for night to fall and bring relief from the brutal heat.

Because my sister was often overwhelmed by Millie's moods, she preferred to withdraw into the blackness, the nowhere of our mother's neglect. I became the attention-seeker, pushing the limits.

But these rare quiet times, when everything was still and safe, were also an opportunity for me to show my colors, to get the responses I needed from my mother. I'd jump up suddenly, pull a cicada from a nearby tree, then terrorize my sister with it. Susan screamed and ran, breaking the treasured calm. My mother, ever enamored of my tricks, laughed heartily, which, of course, pleased me to no end.

Other times, I might choose to let the calmness swallow us, to trust in it more. Then, our mother would suggest we go inside. She'd turn on the air conditioner and start a pot of fudge. Maybe she'd put on one of her favorite albums—Neil Diamond or the Bee Gees. She'd linger near the stereo and start to dance, slowly, alone, magnificent in her beauty, until Susan and I joined her. The three of us, having beaten the heat, were becoming new again, encased in a tiny bubble of safety akin to what I thought others had. On those precious, fleeting days when our mother felt whole, the world didn't seem so threatening.

This is the way we liked to believe our mother really was.

Chapter Two

Surrounded by Enemies: Growing up on Vine Street

Hinsdale, the Chicago suburb where Susan and I grew up for over a decade, was the embodiment of upper-middle-class America—stuffy, hyperaware of the Joneses, and unabashedly bourgeois. Its well-manicured lawns, seemingly badges of pride, reflected the people who kept them, signifying control both inside and out. Hedges were trimmed with great care, children played fairly, and freshly washed family cars rolled slowly and safely by. Order prevailed.

If we kept to ourselves, it seemed possible to fit in, though everyone knew we were the only family on the block without a father. Sometimes, our front lawn might grow over a bit, becoming too untidy for our fastidious neighbors. Before long, one of the men in the neighborhood would come by and, without asking us, mow it.

Millie didn't make friends with the other women in the neighborhood. Instead, she came to be seen as a menace to the block's stability and peace, and Susan and I as threats to the fragile balance of discipline and safety for the neighborhood kids. It often seemed as if we were being whispered about throughout the neighborhood—in backyards, at dinner tables, on street corners.

But there was little actual contact with the neighbors. When we had any at all, it was usually because of some problem. One time, a neighbor sauntered over while Millie was out sunbathing in a bikini and requested that she cover herself. When our mother tanned, she bronzed, her hair grew lighter—glints of blonde highlights reflecting in the sun—and she wore a bright yellow bikini. She was gorgeous, more beautiful than any of the other mothers on our block. One woman, mentioning her two teenage boys, said, "You know how boys can be at that age," hoping Millie would understand. But my mother was not easily reasoned with. Without replying, she stood up, wrapped herself in a towel, and retreated into the house.

In years to come, the neighbors' curiosity about Millie's affairs would send our mother ranting and raving for days, often to the detriment of my sister and me. On bad days, neighborhood boys who stole glances at her sunbathing were spies, and their worried parents were not just nuisances but "ruining" her life.

Millie always tried to avoid such confrontations; when they did occur, she was powerfully affected by them. Inside the house, she paced and brooded, clearing her throat nervously, incessantly. She would smoke several cigarettes, one right after the other, and repeatedly peer out the window, waiting for a safe time to return to her chair in the sun.

Every summer, the same neighbor would say from her yard, "She's at it again," loud enough so our mother could hear, but Millie wasn't always as tough as she seemed. It took her years of sulking inside the house, where no one could see her, to muster the courage to tell the nosy neighbor to leave her alone.

Privacy, for my mother, was as essential as the air she breathed. Though naturally friendly, even gregarious, she would become paralyzed by the paranoia that seemed to increase over the years and that often led to bouts of delusion and rage. Regardless of whether she was ever able, rationally, to assess this side of herself, she consistently acted on it; she kept the world out, and so did we.

Our mother also feared false accusations being leveled at her. If private family information were exposed (as Millie often believed it often was), what would be the consequences? Would she be sent to jail? Lose her children? Suffer something even worse? Growing up like this, we never knew. At an age when our mother's beliefs were gospel, Susan and I didn't attempt to reason with her. Instead, we protected her like warriors, defending her interests, her cherished privacy, and her vulnerability. Unwilling as we may have been, we became inhabitants of her world—a terrifying and unpredictable place to live.

Even the very walls of our house became cause for suspicion. Sometimes, our mother would notice pores so miniscule that, even if I put my nose to them, they were barely perceptible. Slightly textured, the walls were bound to have pores, which is where our mother believed tiny cameras were hidden. And because of this, we were prohibited from saying certain things around the walls. "Shhh!" she'd admonish me if I said too much, like giving away where we were going, or what we'd done earlier that day.

At other times, we weren't even allowed to answer the telephone; she told us it was bugged, our conversations were recorded, "they" were listening. Everywhere we went, we carried a sense that we were being followed and watched. Everyone was a potential spy, had ill intent, or was out to hurt us. As we got older, our mother refused to go to school functions for fear of being followed. The teachers, she said, were spying on her through Susan and me. She became angry about these invasions that we could never actually see or find any evidence of. Several times, Millie thought she smelled gas leaking in the house, and Susan and I feared we'd all go up in flames, but Millie refused to call the gas company. Once, our grandmother called for her, but our mother wouldn't let the serviceman in the house.

Though she was primarily afraid of people, she also feared the germs people spread. If we went to McDonald's, we ate in the car; we were never allowed to use public bathrooms.

I can't recall a time during my childhood when our mother wasn't paranoid. Even her appearance seemed affected by her delusions; it was as if her beauty stemmed from fragility and a sense of danger. The softer side of her paranoia was her vulnerability and the fact that she could easily be taken advantage of.

As she tried to ward off her demons, I felt she was protecting us. One difference between Susan and me, was that I believed my mother, whereas Susan was simply afraid of her. In responding to threats, real or perceived, I mirrored my mother, rarely wondering if anything were wrong with her. I started to think teachers were spying and tiny hidden cameras pressing in upon us. I chose to trust that our mother was caring for us- not so much by clothing and feeding us but by keeping us safe from spies and the cruel world out there. More probably, Millie was protecting us from herself, from her own darkest demons.

While Susan never openly disputed our mother's assertion that tiny cameras were hidden in our walls, I could tell by the way she reacted that she wasn't buying it, and this left me torn between my mother's authority and Susan's judgment.

For Millie, bringing the outside world into our home was very threatening. Inevitably, Susan and I were left to straddle two worlds: the one outside our house, and the one that Millie inhabited. I usually didn't distinguish between the two. Even if we believed, at times, that she was causing us harm, we were too terrified to argue the point.

For Susan and me, this was normal living. If anyone had asked us at the time (which, generally, no one did) if things at home were in any way "unusual," we wouldn't have known how to answer. The more our mother kept the world out, the less Susan and I knew about the world outside. As far as we were concerned, this was everyday life.

When I would venture out, things happened that seemed to validate my mother's concerns— at least in my mind. I used to talk my mother into taking me to the movies, figuring it would do her some good to get out of the house. Susan usually preferred to stay home alone, savoring a quiet break from us. When my mother and I went, we'd see action films like *Deliverance* or the James Bond movie *Live and Let Die*. For days afterward, I was terrified that someone would play Russian roulette with me or that I would be buried alive.

We'd see comedies, too, but these didn't leave much of an impression on me. It was the horror movies, the thrillers, and the spy films that remained in my head. I was often bullied at school and, though I fought back, I feared someone might actually beat me up, ruin my art project, or follow me home. Nothing like that ever happened, but kids at seven or eight can be cruel, and my imagination was active and fertile. Because of the films my mother and I would see, I knew all the myriad ways I could be kidnapped, brutalized, and murdered.

At about that age, I went to visit a neighbor's house. There was a group of girls there, and they were going through the silverware drawer in the kitchen. One of the girls pulled a knife from the drawer and held it up, jokingly pointing it at me. With all the intimidation she could muster, she growled, "I'm going to stab you!" Without missing a beat, I darted off and ran home crying. I pushed my way through the front door, screaming to my mother that the neighbor girl had tried to stab me. My mother didn't for a moment doubt my accusation or stop to ask for details. First making sure I didn't have any knife wounds, she grabbed my hand and marched me back over to the neighbor's. Without knocking, she stormed inside and shouted at the girl's mother for allowing her to play with knives. As uncharacteristic as it was for my mother to take such decisive action, her reality was suddenly confirmed, her reaction appropriate. She was convinced the neighbors were out to get us. Like my mother, I developed a pervasive paranoia.

Susan and I learned, over time, what Millie could manage and what she couldn't. Helping us with our homework, for example, was usually out of her reach. Often, we simply asked her to read instructions. She'd get halfway through, then, clearly exasperated, announce, "I can't do this," and exchange the textbook for a cigarette.

When she did take care of us, it was as if we were being mothered by a young girl, as if we required only the care that dolls did. She'd comb our hair, dry us after a bath, dance with us. This kind of caretaking seemed to come naturally to Millie, whereas cooking, cleaning, and schoolwork were beyond her.

I sensed that my mother was always weary, but I never understood why. As far as I knew, nothing she did during the day, except for the occasional jog, could account for her persistent exhaustion.

Where Millie fell short, Susan and I took over. Millie sometimes went days without food; Susan and I, worried, would try to get her to eat. "Aren't you hungry, Mom?" we'd ask, as if having to introducing the concept of food. "How about if we go to the store tonight?"

Susan fought to make our home more habitable, to create the kind of environment she longed for, a place with stability and routine. She'd wake me up in the morning for school and prepare breakfast while Millie slept. She'd figure out ways to make do with what odds and ends we could find in the cupboards, pouring sugar and orange juice into bowls of stale Cheerios to make them more palatable. We were careful not to disturb Millie while we ate, dressed, packed our bags, and set off for school together. Most days, we arrived for class on time. Often, when we returned home in the afternoons, Millie would still be in bed. If not, she'd be on the couch in front of the television, a cigarette burning in her hand.

As frightening as it was to be around Millie during her descents into fear and irrationality, I still clung to her. Despite her shortcomings, her unusual behavior, she was the only family I had, the only person I felt I could trust. I managed to glean a sense of protection from Millie; I truly thought that things could be far worse. Without her, I feared, I'd have to live inside a different and unfamiliar kind of chaos. Millie's world, even with all its turmoil, was the only world I knew. It was my world.

So as Susan tried to control our environment, I tried to control Millie. These were our unspoken, distinct roles as we struggled to manage our unmanageable lives. We were two children hoping to bridge the chasm between the world outside and our mother's very different version inside. Our efforts were valiant but doomed to fail.

When Susan was in first grade, just learning to write, she began to compose letters to our mother.

> *For you mommy . . . Dear Mommy, We are very very corry cosing so much truddle. Me and tina will do better nekst time. Love Susie and tina.*

And, in a Valentine's Day card a year later, she communicated a similar message:

> *Dear mom, I am carry we cawz to much trubble. I try to help with tina to.*

Susan and I could have, at some point, planned an escape. We might have climbed out a window in the middle of the night or simply not returned home from school one afternoon. If we went through with such a plan, however, we'd eventually have to tell someone, and we were both too terrified of the consequences to do that. Susan and I lacked the language to discuss what we were living—not only with others but even with each other. Without words to make our experiences real, we were mute. What we shared, instead, was the knowledge that we simply couldn't help each other.

Susan once admitted that she was afraid if she told anyone about our lives, Millie would kill her. In bed, at night, we prayed for someone to help us, though I never wished to be taken away from my mother. I prayed for her safe and lasting return from wherever she went in those times when I couldn't reach her. I always knew she was sick and needed help, but there wasn't a name for what caused her so much suffering. Nobody seemed to know what was wrong with her, let alone how to remedy it.

Susan often coped by leaving, heading over to our grandmother's house or finding refuge at a friend's. But I waited for Millie, absorbing her pain, empathizing, trying to think of something to make her happy, hoping to discover what it was that had stolen the life from her.

Chapter Three

Tragedy and Denial: A Family Legacy

My mother, born Mildred Ann Stafford in 1941, came from a long line of privileged, cultured, educated, and stoic women, all of whom firmly believed that children were raised to be "seen and not heard."

Although Millie didn't hold this tradition of stern child-rearing, our grandmother Kathryn did, and we remained close to her while growing up. She lived within a mile of us in an old Victorian home left to her by her second husband.

Of all our friends or relatives, Kathryn saw us most frequently. She sensed that our childhoods were being deeply compromised by Millie's moods and inability to care for us but, maintaining her impassive and aristocratic air, she brushed off much of it. Kathryn had long ago stopped taking the blame for things. Her relationship with her own mother had been marked by extreme bitterness and disillusionment, and she had spent years under a heavy blanket of guilt and searing criticism. She wasn't about to reenact the painful saga with her daughter.

Kathryn did step in where she could, bringing groceries and checking on us once or twice a week. She drove us to Sunday school or took us out for ice cream; she even used her own money to help pay Millie's mortgage or to buy us shoes and school clothes.

With Susan and me, Kathryn deviated—to some extent—from her seen-and-not heard doctrine, trying her best to let us be kids, giving us something of an emotional outlet. This was difficult for her and meant ignoring the bigger picture: the unmistakable signs of Millie's illness.

In the fullest sense of the word, Kathryn was stoic—she even dressed the part. I never remember seeing her wear anything other than pressed linen tops, scratchy wool skirts, nylons, and "smart" but expensive shoes. Everything about her said "nothing in excess," mind your manners and, above all, keep your distance.

This posture toward the world was her bedrock; it formed the basis of her relationship with her children and her husbands and her rearing of Susan and me; she kept the "proper" distance. She never intended to train warriors, but in the frenzy of our lives with Millie—a warrior in her own right—Kathryn became a warrior, too.

Kathryn would often remind me not to ruin my shoes by dragging my feet. She showed me—in public— the proper way for a "lady" to walk: shoulders back, head held high.

One time, Kathryn took Susan and me to an expensive shoe store in Hinsdale. The shoes we'd been wearing were two sizes too small for us, and the clerk asked her, "Why did you wait so long to get them new shoes?" Kathryn nearly fell to pieces in shame, horrified that someone thought that she hadn't "done her duty."

From a very young age, Kathryn was reared as if she were attending charm school. Her mother Ethel instilled in her and her two sisters the importance of education, femininity, grace, and etiquette. As the oldest of the girls, Kathryn learned to sew, bake, and cook; she also became an adept caretaker. She was given Bible lessons; as part of her studies, she learned that cleanliness was next to godliness, a maxim she always upheld. By the age of eight, she was reading novels and poetry; she continued her avid reading, graduating from high school with honors. Kathryn received her bachelor's degree from William Woods College in Missouri and, in 1932 a master's in English from Beloit College in Wisconsin. Then she attended the prestigious Presbyterian Hospital School of Nursing in Chicago.

Her sister Margaret dropped out of college and married a farmer, which greatly upset Kathryn. In the years to come, however, she happily sent her own children to her sister's farm in Roanoke, Illinois, for vacations. Millie spent blissful summers there, enjoying the relaxed atmosphere of the farm and the company of her aunt and cousins, feeling part of a family.

Kathryn's other sister, Libby, became a schoolteacher but spent a great deal of her time caring for Ethel. Though she married briefly in her younger years, Libby remained single most of her life and retired early from teaching to take care of her mother full-time. Libby was known for her eccentricity; while riding around town on her bicycle, she would continually stop to look back, afraid someone was following her.

Libby was a favorite of Susan's and mine. She'd come to Kathryn's for Sunday dinner, and always seemed spirited and warm. But when she inexplicably stopped showing up, Kathryn and I began going to her apartment with groceries or to check on her. We'd stand at her door, knowing Libby was inside, and knock. "Libby, dear," Kathryn said softly. "Libby, open the door please. It's your sister Kate." Sometimes, Libby slowly opened the door and peeked out with one eye. It took a lot of convincing for Kathryn to get into the apartment to deliver the food. Often, we were forced to leave Libby's groceries in the outside hallway.

Libby once traveled from Detroit to Chicago. At the Chicago station though, she adamantly refused to get off the train. When the crew tried to coax her off, she became hysterical. They had to call a family member to get her off the train. At the time, the family viewed Libby's behavior as strange, unique to her; in retrospect, it seems to have been an illness and a harbinger of things to come.

Kathryn did well in nursing, a profession that suited her. In fact, even years after she stopped working, something in Kathryn's demeanor suggested she was always "on duty." She seemed more comfortable dealing with the world from a safe, professional distance.

After working several years at Presbyterian Hospital, she met Charles Arthur Stafford, a surgical resident at the medical center. In 1939, while rehearsing for a play to raise money for tuberculosis research, they fell in love and, shortly thereafter, became engaged.

Charles' job took him to Cheyenne, Wyoming, where Kathryn enjoyed much time away on vacation getting periodic respites from her overbearing mother. Charles and Kathryn were married in 1941, and Charles went on to become a renowned surgeon, giving Kathryn the opportunity to live without requiring the financial support from her family, which often made her feel guilty and indebted to them. Later that year, Kathryn became pregnant with Millie.

Unfortunately, however, Kathryn's safe haven away from Hinsdale was fleeting. During their engagement, in 1939, Charles had joined the U.S. Army Medical Reserve. Later, he was commissioned a first lieutenant in the regular army and, in 1941, was promoted to captain. Upon completion of his training at the School of Aviation Medicine at Randolph Field in San Antonio, Texas, Charles qualified as an aviation medical examiner. He was then posted at the station hospital at Fort Douglas, Utah. Following the attack on Pearl Harbor

Charles & Millie, just before he left in 1941

in December 1941, the United States entered the Second World War; Charles was assigned to the 9th Bombardment Group and attached to one of its squadrons in the South Pacific. Kathryn was forced to take Millie, just under a year old, back to Hinsdale to live with her mother until Charles returned home.

On April 4, 1942, Kathryn received a letter from Mabel Stafford, Charles' mother:

Dear Kathryn,

Got your letter this morning—we have had no further news, but I feel sure I'll hear from him—I refuse to think any other way.

The telegram read, "We regret to inform you that your son, Capt. Charles Arthur Stafford has been missing in action in a far eastern theatre of war since March 3rd. Further information will be wired as soon as received."

They announced over the radio not to bother them with requests for more information since they are getting it as fast as possible—however you do as like about it.

I had a note from Para and a note from South Africa—then a phone call from Java but nothing more. He hadn't received any of my letters at that time. I've written once a week or oftener.

The weather is grand here now—a beautiful Easter for once I guess.

Yes, this year is terrible and I'm afraid only starting.

Hope Mildred Ann is better.

If I get any information I'll forward it immediately but it may be months on when the war is over.

Love,
Mother

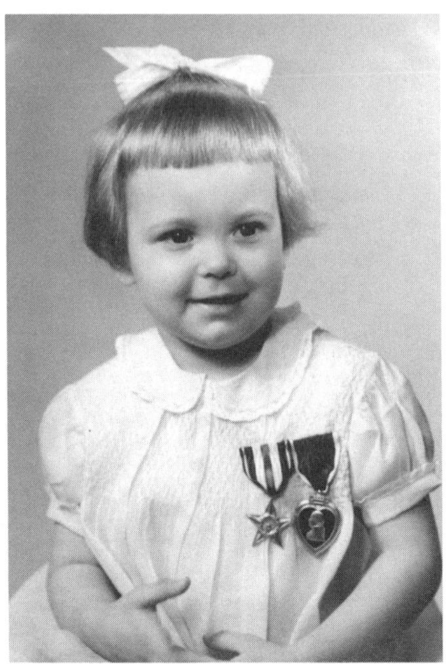

Millie age 2 1/2, with her father's Silver Star and Purple Heart

On April 24, 1942, Kathryn received a telegram informing her that Charles had died on March 3 while tending to a wounded soldier; his plane went down off the coast of Broome, Australia. His body was never recovered. One month later, Kathryn received a special delivery containing the Purple Heart and Silver Star awarded to Charles posthumously.

Kathryn, still living with her mother, had little space to grieve. True to form she remained stoic and kept it together for the sake of Millie. Though receiving a small widow's pension, Kathryn needed to find a way to support herself, so she returned to work part-time at Presbyterian Hospital. She remained active in the community, taking Millie to choir lessons at the local church, visiting with friends and neighbors. She carried a profound pain for the rest of her life but she did so alone, never speaking of it.

Though she was fairly soft-spoken and shy, Kathryn had always turned heads. She had a classic beauty—fair skin, long auburn hair—and considerable sophistication and elegance. Eventually, Kathryn attracted the attention of a local man. Though divorced and ten years older than Kathryn, John Hall was charming, well-bred, and gainfully employed. He fell in love with both Kathryn and Millie and was ready to start a new family. John's son Wes, who had already graduated college at that point, was pleasant, well-educated, and clearly had the proper upbringing that Kathryn wished for Millie.

Millie simply adored her new stepfather-to-be. Like her, he was a nature lover, and he kindly regarded the armloads of animals she brought home—the rabbit that had babies in her bed, the caterpillars she let hatch along the drapery, and all the stray kittens she could find. He loved to take her fishing, and he delighted in the nature walks they took together. In 1944, Kathryn and John were wed.

A year later, Kathryn gave birth to a second child, John. Millie quickly became a proud and doting big sister, carrying John wherever she went, playing with him, and reading to him while Kathryn did housework.

Together, Kathryn and John were strict, protective, but loving parents. The four of them made a happy family.

But during the summer of 1954, during a family vacation in Wisconsin, John Sr., went to see a doctor about a lesion on his calf that wouldn't heal. The doctor said it was serious and immediately sent him to Presbyterian Hospital, where he was diagnosed with leukemia. Kathryn kept the news from her children, simply saying that their father "wasn't feeling well."

Kathryn trudged on, terrified but determined, raising her two children, but now spending long days at the hospital with her husband. By this time, Millie was a teenager and John was nine.

In the ensuing months, Kathryn grew lonely and depressed. Pushing aside her children's questions about their father, she did not allow them to visit him in the hospital for fear they would transmit germs to him. Perhaps she felt that by keeping Millie and John away from their dying father, she could protect them from the pain and loss. However, this imposed distance took its toll, and Kathryn paved the way for denial and isolation, both for herself and for her children. She hadn't been getting support from her family—neither her mother nor her sisters—and she wasn't one to ask for it.

Millie, who had been taking care of her younger brother while her mother spent long days at the hospital, began having outbursts. She was mature and sensitive enough to notice Kathryn's deep depression. She worried about her mother but had no real outlet for expressing her fear and anger. Though she knew some of what was happening to her stepfather, what she understood most clearly was that his illness was wrecking her mother's happiness.

Occasionally, John would be released from the hospital so that Kathryn could take care of him at home. One day Millie, just home from school, encountered her stepfather in the kitchen.

"You know, Millie, I'm dying," he said to her. Millie replied, "I don't care."

Clearly, this wasn't what she'd been feeling, but she'd already started to build a shell in an attempt to survive.

Millie began to yell at her parents, often for no clear reason. Kathryn was always deeply embarrassed by Millie's behavior, so she dealt quietly with her outbursts; she was too consumed with her own pain at the time to deal with Millie's. The tension in the house was terrible, and John Jr. avoided going home after school. When he did arrive, he took his meals in front of the television or in his room. He may have understood less than Millie did about what was happening to his father, but he, too, was alone with his pain. It wasn't until forty years later that he ever spoke about what he'd felt.

In 1955, John Sr. returned to the hospital for the final time. He passed away in the middle of the night, Kathryn and Wes at his side, from complications of acute leukemia. His illness, from diagnosis until death, lasted six months. When Millie woke up in the morning, Kathryn and Wes gave her the news of her stepfather's death. Wes then woke John Jr., saying simply, "Time to get up. Dad died."

Kathryn, widowed for the second time, her dreams of raising children in a loving, two-parent home shattered, continued to keep her feelings locked away. Life went on, but the next few years proved difficult for the entire family. Ethel became so bitter and demanding that Kathryn rarely went to see her. As in the past, Kathryn had no one to turn to for support.

Fortunately, John Sr. had provided for the family to keep their home; it was there that Kathryn raised the two children by herself.

During her first year at the local high school, the year after her stepfather died, Millie's grades took a turn for the worse; they were below average to failing. She began hanging out with "the wrong crowd" and testing her mother's boundaries, seemingly attempting to get at the emotions Kathryn had always refused to acknowledge.

When Millie turned sixteen, Kathryn, concerned about her daughter's behavior and extreme lethargy, took Millie to a doctor. The doctor diagnosed Millie with hypothyroidism and put her on Synthroid, a hormone-replacement medication that had just come on the market. However, Millie's symptoms—which appeared to Kathryn to be signs of depression— didn't improve.

One day at end of the summer before Millie's sophomore year in high school, she came home with a friend and found her mother loading the car. Kathryn had taken all of Millie's belongings and packed them into suitcases: she told Millie to get in the car. Along with a neighbor, Kathryn drove Millie to Wayland Academy, a strict co-ed boarding school in Wisconsin that prided itself on proper etiquette and education. When they arrived at the school, the two women got out of the car, opened the trunk, and took out the suitcases; Kathryn summarily informed Millie that this was where she would live from now on.

Kathryn's sister Margaret couldn't understand why Kathryn wanted to send Millie away. They fought about it bitterly, and Kathryn confessed she couldn't handle Millie's behavior. Concluding that Kathryn couldn't handle much of anything, Margaret offered to take Millie to live with her on her farm. Although Millie seemed to thrive whenever she visited the farm as a child, Kathryn lied to Margaret, saying Millie didn't want to live with her. Kathryn also told Millie not to involve herself any longer with Margaret and her family. "They're a family of complainers," she declared. "Don't get involved. Better to stay neutral." Kathryn felt her daughter would benefit more from the structured environment (and relative sterility) of boarding school.

But that environment—where nylons were required and overbearing teachers rated students on their attire and manners—was extremely humiliating for Millie, and she quickly grew more lonely and withdrawn. During one of Millie's visits home, John returned from baseball practice to find his mother pinned to the floor by his sister in a furious rage. A window had been kicked out: Millie was screaming at Kathryn and hitting her. John managed to pull Millie away and contain her. From then on, Millie and John slowly became strangers to one another, with Kathryn at the crux of their alienation. John, tired of the anger and fear that Millie carried and caused, was relieved when Millie returned to boarding school.

Due to the stress of her first year at boarding school, Millie started gaining weight and developed a smoking habit. During one of Millie's school vacations, Kathryn took her to a doctor who prescribed Dexedrine, a "diet pill."

Today, Dexedrine is more commonly prescribed in cases of attention-deficit disorder and narcolepsy, but it was often used for weight loss at the time, and eventually Millie became addicted to the drug. Dexedrine is a stimulant, and its withdrawal effects often include severe depression and fatigue; hence, the high risk for dependence. Because of the tolerance factor, increased dosage is required with prolonged use to maintain the same level of efficacy, making it possible that Millie could have experienced toxicity from overuse of the drug. Side effects of Dexedrine overdose can include restlessness, insomnia, and even a psychosis clinically indistinguishable from schizophrenia.

When Kathryn noticed Millie's behavior becoming more strange and erratic, she decided to take her daughter to a psychiatrist, Dr. Swanson, whom Millie would continue to see, off and on, for the next twenty years.

Eventually, Kathryn transferred Millie to a more relaxed boarding school: Monticello School for Girls in Alton, Illinois—but with the stipulation that she couldn't return home for weekends unless she had the money to pay her own train fare.

Instead, Millie began visiting Margaret's farm on her time off from school. Margaret stayed in touch with Millie, sending care packages from time to time. Millie's new situation proved to be markedly better than the Wisconsin school. Her grades during her junior and senior years improved; she made friends and joined the Spanish club and the glee club. At the end of her senior year, she was elected the class beauty in the school's yearbook.

In 1959, at eighteen, Millie graduated with high marks and was accepted to Drake University in Des Moines, Iowa. She hadn't wanted to go to college, but her stepbrother Wes, whom Millie had always admired, emphasized that college meant opportunities she wouldn't have if she stuck around at home.

Almost immediately, her grades showed that her heart wasn't in it. Her stepbrother again intervened, helping her transfer to the University of Illinois. There, closer to her mother and home, Millie felt more secure and continued with her studies, majoring in health education and minoring in biology. Despite her intellectual ability, she was easily distracted, so she started taking more Dexedrine to keep up with her schoolwork and maintain her focus.

Millie's charm, sense of humor, and beauty attracted both friends and would-be suitors at Illinois and kept her from feeling totally alienated. However, a persistent loneliness troubled her and, after just six months, she was expelled because of failing grades. She returned home, hoping to find a reprieve from the feelings she associated with being alone in the world, away from what was familiar to her.

However, once home, Millie found little solace. Kathryn noticed, for the first time, that Millie simply lacked the drive to succeed. She attributed it to acute shyness; she encouraged Millie to push beyond her natural limits and return to school in hope of finding a career—maybe even a husband.

At twenty-one, Millie moved back to school, determined to pick up where she had left off. She chose to pursue nursing, as her mother and her mother's mother had.

About a year later, in a health education class, Millie met the man she would eventually marry.

Chapter Four

Love Amid Broken Dreams

Alan Smiley was raised in a middle-class Jewish family. Serious-minded and hard-working, he studied constantly, which helped him avoid his father Morrie, who was often harsh and domineering.

Alan graduated from high school six months early because his family moved out of the school district. He got early acceptance at the University of Illinois, hoping to one day join the Peace Corps and go on to study law. A talented running back in high school, Alan made the Illinois football team as a "walk-on."

As an undergrad, while pursuing a degree in physical education, he met Millie; they were immediately attracted to each other. In Alan's eyes, Millie—articulate, studious, and beautiful—clearly stood out from the crowd. Millie found Alan to be intelligent, health-conscious, and more mature than most of the other guys, who were mainly interested in partying.

Only three months after they started dating, Millie became pregnant. With great trepidation, she broke the news to Alan during a picnic. The following weeks were a horrible time of uncertainty and shock; her depression, which continued to go unnoticed by everyone around her, deepened.

Alan considered the situation carefully, then gave Millie three options: have an abortion, go away for the duration of the pregnancy and give up the baby for adoption, or marry him. Millie sensed that Alan had no desire to get married at that time, and the thought of going away terrified her, bringing back memories of her boarding-school days.

Kathryn and Alan's parents soon found out about the pregnancy. Morrie, who had yet to meet Millie, used Yiddish words to express his strong feelings on the matter. He called Alan a *meshugener* (a crazy man) for messing around with a *shikse* (a non-Jewish woman).

But when at last they met, Millie adored Morrie, whom she found charmingly forthright. She loved his sense of humor and delighted in having dinner with Alan's parents so she could listen to his jokes. Millie always admired a keen wit; laughter to her was the best medicine. She didn't mind being teased and quickly learned the Yiddish terms Morrie often used at the dinner table.

Despite the fact that—or perhaps because—she'd never been very religious, she converted to Judaism at the Smiley's request. Though she and Alan never practiced except at holidays and family events, Millie felt her conversion brought her closer to Alan's family. It also drove her further from Kathryn who, as a longtime member of the Union Church of Hinsdale, was very unhappy with Millie's decision.

Though Morrie enjoyed Millie's company and was pleased that she chose the faith of his family, Alan continued to remain alienated from his father. When relations became particularly strained, Millie could sense Alan's deep unhappiness and the pain of his thwarted dreams. She was overwhelmed by trying to make a decision that both she and Alan could live with.

Finally, she decided to have an abortion. A mutual friend loaned Millie and Alan several hundred dollars, the fee that a local chiropractor charged to perform the procedure. It was 1963, ten years before the landmark *Roe v. Wade* decision.

One afternoon, Millie and Alan entered a small office on the top floor of a dreary building in Champaign, Illinois. The chiropractor examined Millie, then simply said, "I can't do it. You have too many folds in your uterus." She walked out, relieved.

Clearly, things weren't going to turn out as Alan planned, and he asked Millie to marry him. When Millie was about four months pregnant, they decided to elope. They drove to Michigan, where eighteen was the age of majority and, on May 25, 1963, they were married by a justice of the peace in New Buffalo. Alan accepted his new responsibilities, but he was devastated.

Millie's performance in school had been steadily deteriorating; on the advice of her mother, she quit in order to rest during her pregnancy. She moved back into Kathryn's house, where her brother John was still living while attending school. Meanwhile, Alan stayed in student housing and hurried to graduate. When he finished, he also moved to Kathryn's. John and Alan didn't get along at all, so the arrangement lasted only briefly.

Against Kathryn's wishes, Millie and Alan moved to an apartment in Champaign. Millie had some savings bonds from her grandmother and a pension she received from the government as a war orphan. She cashed in these assets and, for a time, they were able to support themselves.

Though Kathryn knew Millie was in love with Alan, she ultimately opposed the marriage, as did the rest of the family. Wes felt that Alan couldn't be a good provider with only a degree in physical education; he also worried that Alan wasn't prepared for the commitment he had made to Millie. John never liked Alan, saying he was "just a charmer."

The antipathy was mutual; Alan clearly resented Kathryn's involvement in their lives and the influence she had on Millie. Alan seemed to think Kathryn encouraged Millie to "feed off" him. He told Millie he thought she was becoming lazy, and this only served to exacerbate Millie's depression. So, as much as he could, Alan kept his distance from Millie's family.

Millie struggled to remain cheerful during the pregnancy, and

Kathryn tried to offer her daughter everything she could, except real emotional support—which Millie desperately needed at a time when her life was changing drastically. Alan had to become the sole breadwinner in the family and, with his own set of worries and all his hopes pushed aside, the tension between him and Millie increased. Millie began to feel like a burden.

Years later, Alan said that, while pregnant with Susan, Millie often became despondent but that he assumed her moods were caused by hormonal changes. Photos and home movies from that time show Millie, stunning even in the later months of her pregnancy, looking away from the camera, far off, seemingly unreachable.

Physically, though, Millie remained healthy and, on October 26, 1963, in Urbana, Illinois, she gave birth to Susan.

Although Alan was delighted by the birth of Susan, any remaining dreams for himself vanished the moment she was born, and the reality of his situation affected him deeply. With his degree in physical health education, he found a job as a phys-ed teacher at a junior high school in Monticello, where he and Millie began renting a house. Eventually, Alan started working longer hours,

Millie and Alan, 1964

seemingly to avoid going home to Millie. He had just finished college and his job paid very little, so, during the summer months, he augmented his salary by working at a steelworks factory.

Millie, too, was overwhelmed and unhappy. She had a newborn baby, a husband who seemed to be avoiding her, and precious little support. She was depressed and listless and couldn't explain why she was sleeping most of the time. When Alan would return home, he'd find Millie in bed, Susan crying in diapers that hadn't been changed all day. Millie sensed Alan's disappointment in her; this ate away at her self-esteem, deepened her depression, and caused Alan to withdraw from her even more.

There were many times when Millie was truly delusional with Alan, lashing out at him for no apparent reason. She was frightened and acted strangely, and Alan had no context to understand Millie's erratic behavior. He regarded these episodes as lingering hormonal imbalances or perhaps attitudinal problems—a "bitchy streak." When Alan criticized Millie—her sanity, her housekeeping, her ability as a mother—she grew more intimidated and (as Susan and I experienced when we got older) began to withhold her rage until it was beyond control.

When Morrie and Anne, Alan's parents, came to visit Millie and the new baby, they brought an entire carload of groceries. Millie was overjoyed, not only by the food but also by the support that accompanied it. Following the visit by Alan's family, she and Alan went to her Aunt Margaret's farm for two weeks, where they were both able, finally, to get some much-needed rest.

However, a mere three weeks after Susan was born, when the excitement and the visits were over, Millie, home alone, tried to kill herself by slitting her wrists.

When Alan found her, Millie was in the fetal position under the blankets of their bed. The pillows and sheets were covered in blood.

The apartment was a mess and Susan had not been attended to for some time. They barely exchanged a word. He simply bandaged her up and never mentioned the incident.

Alan avoided telling his family; it's likely he was afraid of their reaction if they found out he'd married such an unstable woman. Years later, when Susan interviewed him for *Out of the Shadow*, a documentary she filmed about our mother, he said simply of that time with Millie: "I felt terribly alone."

In that same interview, he told Susan that, though he was proud to be a father, he was not proud to be married to Millie and more than a little disgusted. "She wasn't working with a full deck." He explained that she became despondent for long periods and that, eventually, he was no longer able to reach her at all. He said he'd spoken, on occasion, with a few of his former college professors about Millie's suicide attempt but with no one else. When Millie tried to kill herself after giving birth, Alan knew he would leave her; it was only a matter of time. He said she was never the same after her pregnancy, that she was never "whole" again.

As Millie's mental health declined, Alan began preparing for his escape. The situation between them quickly turned ugly. If Millie's sense of threat became heightened, if her rationality failed her, so did Alan's. It was as if they were fueling each other's behavior. Perhaps because of Alan's pride and likely because of his own fears, he could not step back enough to recognize that he'd been feeding Millie's depression by avoiding her and by not letting up with his own anger toward her. Millie was unable to turn things around, either; fights escalated in frequency and ferocity.

After the suicide attempt, Alan arranged to return Millie to her family, where he felt she could get the care she needed. He began to save money to buy a house close to Kathryn's. He realized that even though the situation wasn't ideal for Millie, who felt suffocated in the presence of her mother, Kathryn could offer her support. Alan was still in his early twenties, sacrificing his dreams for a baby girl and a woman who was not only distant but also suicidal. He had clear reasons for leaving; this was not what he'd bargained for.

Using earnings from work along with Millie's remaining savings bonds, Alan placed a down payment on a house on Vine Street in Hinsdale, one mile from Kathryn.

Soon after they moved into their new home, Millie became pregnant with me. She knew the news would make Alan "fly off the handle." However, if anything, Alan was forced to stick around longer than he intended. Nonetheless, within a year after my birth in March 1966, the marriage had completely crumbled.

While they were still married, Alan took Millie to a company Christmas party, which is where Millie first saw Nancy, the woman Alan would later marry. Although Millie stopped trying to salvage the marriage after that, she did go to a psychiatrist for support—Dr. Swanson, the same one Kathryn had taken her to ten years before. Alan had always wanted her to "buck up and deal with things," and she hoped that the doctor could help alleviate her anxiety about her strained marriage and her decreased ability to do simple tasks around the house.

Our father Alan holding Susan and I, April 1966

This time, Dr. Swanson referred her to a colleague of his. Although much of Millie's medical history, especially from the sixties and seventies, is no longer available, there's evidence this new psychiatrist prescribed Stelazine, a major tranquilizer and antipsychotic. If Millie couldn't get out of bed before, she certainly couldn't once she began taking Stelazine.

People on Stelazine need to be carefully monitored by their physicians, but Millie often decided to take her health into her own hands. She'd go long periods without returning to her doctor, or she'd go back for something else without informing the doctor she was still taking a previous prescription.

After giving birth to me, her obstetrician prescribed Dexedrine for weight loss and to give her a "boost" in the morning. Fortunately, by the time she started Dexedrine, she stopped taking Stelazine; the interaction could have resulted in more weight gain and even psychosis. During a brief visit with her cousin Nancy, Millie told her that the Stelazine was causing "terrible twitching"—a Parkinson's-like symptom that's often a side effect associated with the medication. When Susan and I were younger, our mother's leg was always swinging as she sat on the couch in front of the television, clearing her throat repeatedly with a cigarette in one hand and the fingers of her other hand seemingly moving on their own.

At this time, Millie became increasingly dependent on prescription drugs, often without sufficient monitoring. For tension headaches, she began taking Fiorinal, which contains a barbiturate and tends to worsen depression and increase drowsiness and can disrupt sugar metabolism. That she was also given Darvon, a highly addictive painkiller, whose use was limited in the late eighties because of too many deaths due to overdose—including the highly publicized death of NFL great John Matuszak—is a clear indication of how negligent her doctors were in monitoring Millie while doling out medication to her.

Elavil, a tricyclic antidepressant, Thorazine, another antipsychotic (which likely brought on the leg cramps she suffered from for years), the benzodiazepines Librium and Valium (a heavily prescribed tranquilizer often referred to as "mother's little helper"), and Synthroid, for low-functioning thyroid, could have made for a deadly cocktail. In this case, it was fortunate that Millie didn't take her medications as prescribed.

Shortly after Millie began taking these medications, along with sleeping pills and Benadryl, this colleague of Dr. Swanson lost his license and disappeared.

Without Millie's medical records from this period, it's hard to be certain, but it seems likely that most doctors she saw during this time treated her for anxiety, depression and, occasionally, what they must have perceived to be psychosis. However, no one—not her obstetrician, her internist or her psychiatrist—ever seemed to look at the whole picture of her medical and emotional health.

One day in January 1968, Susan recalls that Alan simply packed his things and left the house. With his bags on his shoulders, he bent over to kiss Susan as she sat on the floor. "Goodbye," he said. "I love you."

Once it was clear that Alan would not be returning, Kathryn began to make daily appearances at our house, helping Millie take care of us, bringing groceries, and providing money for mortgage payments.

In December 1968, with the benefit of the counsel of her brother Wes, Millie filed for divorce on the grounds of mutual and irreconcilable differences. In February 1969, the divorce was finalized. Two months later, Alan married Nancy, the woman Millie first saw at his company Christmas party.

About a year after leaving us, Alan began to suspect that the child support money that he'd been sending wasn't being used for Susan and me. He said that we would come to his house "disheveled, unclean, [in] old clothes." So he and Nancy decided to seek full custody from Millie.

But the process proved difficult. First, at that time, children nearly always remained with their mother after a divorce. Second, Kathryn was vehemently opposed to letting him take us away from Millie; she believed that if he succeeded in winning custody, Millie would never see us again. Alan argued that Kathryn was merely protecting herself because she didn't want to be financially responsible for Millie if her children were taken from her. "So," as he later told Susan, "now you have a woman, a grandmother who, for her own interest, sacrificed her grandchildren to a life of a psychotic—of a psychotic home."

Worn down by the obstacles, Alan eventually gave up pursuing custody, and Millie found herself unable to support the three of us on the money he was sending.

Of course, Millie was far from frugal with the money she was receiving from Alan. She managed our finances terribly. She could be like a child, blowing her "allowance" on expensive shoes rather than buying needed groceries. Millie would cash the checks Alan sent, then the money seemed to disappear. Even when she wasn't spending the money, she was often incapable of focusing long enough to pay the bills on time. Kathryn tried to guide Millie at first but eventually had to take over her financial affairs completely.

Years later, Alan would explain to us that he had to save himself. "If I am going to save anybody, it's going to be me." He explained that Susan and I weren't brought into a family, but rather into "an environment of absolute chaos." He said he left because that was the plan; he'd bought Millie a house and thereby tried to provide some financial stability. "You have to protect yourself emotionally . . . even though you may be sacrificing your loved ones, your children, in this particular case. You have to cut bait and then accept that decision. And don't falter going, because what you're doing is making it worse."

Millie, only twenty-seven, was utterly miserable about the divorce and overwhelmed by her new role as a single parent. "I was lost without your father," she told me once. "Just devastated." One afternoon, she called her mother and told her she was experiencing chest pains. Kathryn, concerned about possible pneumonia, immediately took her to Presbyterian St. Luke's Hospital in Chicago, despite Millie's reluctance.

When Millie was admitted, she had a blood clot in her lung and was treated with anticoagulants. Apparently, however, she was soon transferred to the psychiatric ward. According to Millie, she was acting "strange" and couldn't control herself. She believes it was due to the abrupt stoppage of some of her medications while she was in the hospital.

While she was at Presbyterian St. Luke's, Millie got some more prescriptions. Along with Coumadin for the blood clot, she was given Haldol, one of the most powerful of the antipsychotic drugs—not to be not to be used indiscriminately.

When prescribed for Millie, Haldol had just been introduced in the United States. Within a few years, its use was widespread, as it was considered a significant improvement over older antipsychotics. By the seventies, doctors routinely prescribed Haldol in hospitals, not only to combat psychosis but also to calm unwilling patients. So common was Haldol that it was ironically nicknamed "vitamin H," indicating its omnipresence in locked wards of the time as well as the view of harried employees of understaffed wards that, like vitamins B and C, every patient needed a dose a day. Needless to say, it wasn't a very prudent choice to send home with a single mother.

Many long-time psychiatric patients are fearful of the drug, and those who take it for a prolonged period can develop muscle tremors and impaired movement. Serious consequences, including tardive dyskinesia, an irreversible condition in which patients suffer from involuntary muscle movements, resulted from indiscriminate Haldol use.

Despite its side effects, Haldol is still commonly used, especially in hospital settings. When prescribed for outpatients, the drug is often administered in a long-acting injectable form, which eliminates concerns about compliance and overdosage. Most patients on

Haldol, like Millie, have little insight into why or how they should take the drug and are typically more aware of its side effects than of any benefits.

The fact that she was given Haldol at this time suggests that she was exhibiting clear signs of psychosis. It also indicates that doctors were treating individual symptoms and not concerning themselves with the big picture.

After spending a week in the psychiatric ward of Presbyterian St. Luke's, Millie returned home even more terrified. She knew she wouldn't be able to raise two children alone, and she was still heart-broken by Alan's leaving and the failure of their marriage.

Although I spent only a brief period of my early life with my father, in years to come, I would attempt, repeatedly, to forge a relationship with him. But I came, at last, to understand that he saw me as a shadow of my mother, a haunting reminder of his missteps with her, the "wasted" years of their marriage during which they failed to connect and he was forced to defer his dreams. In his eyes, I was crazy like her. The fear that my father was right stayed with me for years. Would I end up like my mother? Would I eventually suffer as she did for years?

When I'd visit my father, he didn't like anyone to even mention Millie. If she came up in conversation, Alan's typical reaction was to grunt. "Your mother's crazy," he used to say. "Your mother is a lunatic."

"You make choices," Alan said in later years. "My choice was to forget them. From my point of view, she's history. And I have absolutely no sympathy for anything that happens to this woman or her family. Because what they had done was sacrifice my offspring to perpetuate illness and perpetuate what their morality may be at the time, and that's protect the image of 'there's no mental illness here; we're okay.' To hell with them. They all rot in hell."

Chapter Five

Hostages to Her Moods

After our father left, life at our house became strange and somber. Millie would sit on the couch, staring off in a daze, her leg swinging frantically, smoking, clearing her throat repeatedly. When Millie was in one of her "trances," she could remain on the couch for hours. She looked at us without blinking—a cold, hard stare as if she were looking through us. Then, without warning, she might start yelling, ranting, kicking more wildly, as if at any moment she would stand up and come after us with a belt or rolled-up newspaper, which she always kept on the footrest next to the couch. Sometimes, she'd just sit there, snapping the belt, warning us to stay away.

When Millie did start shouting, it was too late to intervene. She'd tell each of us what she hated most about us. Susan was a "botched abortion;" I was an "awful, awful" baby—our father had actually left because I was so intolerable and that he would have preferred a son, instead of another daughter. Sometimes, continuing to rant, she'd follow us to our rooms, screaming at our closed doors until, finally, she was either satisfied she'd been heard or she was exhausted. Other times, when she yelled at us, her exclamations were inexplicable.

A typical episode might go something like this. I'd be playing quietly next to Millie while she sat on the couch in front of the television. Suddenly, she'd sit bolt upright, tense, sensing an immediate "threat." Sometimes, it was from the walls, through the tiny, imperceptible pores, sometimes from the cracks in the floorboards—anything that could let something in from the outside.

"Quiet!" she'd snap. Then she'd look around as if she'd heard something. "Tina, Tina, stop," she'd insist. "They're watching. Stop."

"What do you mean, watching? Who is watching?"

"Sit down and be quiet. Don't move."

I'd look out the window, afraid to find someone peering in, but I'd see no one. At that point, I'd become fearful that, at any moment, someone would burst in with a knife or a shotgun, as often happened in the movies I'd seen with Millie. I'd sit next to her on the couch, quietly waiting until she'd forgotten we were supposed to be still, waiting until "they" weren't watching us anymore.

What could have possibly brought her to such a place of terror when everything, just moments before, had seemed all right? Events long past, lingering fears, and past wrongs were dredged up as if they were occurring that very moment. Alan was wretched; Kathryn was overbearing; her troubles were Susan's or my fault. How could we have done this to her? As I got older, I began to wonder if she might even be drunk, though there was never any alcohol in the house, and I never saw her take a drink.

Millie's anger could sometimes be traced to what seemed like legitimate circumstances—things anyone could get angry about. Other times, it was simply the ring of a telephone that set her off, or a comment a neighbor had made years back. But her response, her expression of anger, was always way out of proportion to the apparent cause. She'd brood until the matter escalated in her mind. Then, suddenly, she'd become overly sensitive to light, to noise, to motion;

she'd go on this way for days until the anger turned to rage, until the only thing that would make the rage subside was lashing out. Her attacks—emotional and physical—became her defense against fear, and they seemed to have a purgative effect on her.

During these tirades, it was as if her enemy were actually in the room with her. She'd look up suddenly and let out a string of profanities, grit her teeth, and clench her fists. Right there before us, our mother's delicate features, her otherwise timid and soft-spoken manner, would be transformed. The tendons and muscles in her body protruded and hardened with rage, and her face took on the crazed and desperate appearance of someone fighting for her very life.

Once she had released all the tension brewing inside her, she became calm again. Sometimes the energy expended would simply exhaust her to the point where she could go on sleeping for days. But when my mother yelled at people who weren't in the room, I felt terrified and ashamed. Because she believed that people were always looking in on us, I assumed they knew when she was acting this way and figured that was why people didn't visit us often.

I remember coming home from school one day and seeing my mother frozen in front of the TV, like a child riveted by a favorite cartoon. Suddenly, she began pacing and muttering profanities. She'd become interested in animal rights at a time when the whole country was in an uproar about the mistreatment of wolves, whales, and other endangered species. Even though she'd never gotten involved in activism per se, there was no mistaking her fervor and fury. She watched, in rapt concern and disgust, the images of Greenpeace members spray-painting the white fur of baby harp seals to save them from being clubbed. "These hunters should be clubbed on the head and shot . . . Ugly disgusting human beings killing innocent creatures. How could someone kill these babies?"

When the mesmerizing stories ended, she'd remain there, motionless, haunted by what she'd seen, dwelling incessantly on the injustice. The intense emotional response drained her; eventually, she crumpled down on the couch and lit a cigarette, my presence in the room unnoticed.

However, Millie's collapse into seeming exhaustion wasn't always a sure indicator that she was through; many times, she would rise and resume her harangue. I'd wait her out, perched right next to her, not saying a word, transfixed and worried right until the end.

I couldn't understand how the welfare of Susan and me came second to that of Millie's beloved animals. This question turned over and over inside my head, slowly beginning to eat away at me.

I remember times when I'd be playing in our backyard, the images of baby harp seals being clubbed to death burning in my mind, waiting for the chance to catch someone who threatened anything—or anyone—innocent. One day, I found a neighborhood boy throwing stones at squirrels. I ran over to him and told him to stop, but he ignored me. Finally, I grabbed the largest rock I could find and threw it at him; to my dismay, it hit him right in the head. He ran home crying, and I ran in the other direction, terrified that his parents would come after me. I eventually returned home and confessed to my mother what I'd done. "He got what he deserved," she said evenly, seeming to encourage my vigilante approach to defending the innocent.

Particularly in the years immediately after the divorce, Millie was very sensitive to "intruders"—the people she believed were coming after us, her "enemies": Kathryn (for meddling in her affairs, for being too overbearing), Alan (for his coldness, for his insensitivity), Susan (for going to visit Alan). Even the postman's delivery of a package, if at the "wrong" time, could seem to Millie a deliberate intrusion, something that would interrupt her "concentration." At times like this, I would get the distinct sense that Millie was upset with people who'd actually disturbed her while she was alone. After several years of finding no evidence that anyone had been in the house while we were gone and knowing Millie had likely been sleeping most of the day, I realized her stories just didn't add up.

For a long time, she saw all men the way she saw our father, and often she would go off on tirades about them. If she were out in public and had to interact with a man, even at the grocery store checkout, she'd become upset, sometimes terribly so, but she'd wait until we got back into the car, or even back home, to tell Susan and me that men were "despicable" and "filthy."

When Millie was withdrawn and depressed, our house was always dark. The curtains would remain closed for days. The living room, where she spent much of her time in front of the television, had two picture windows that faced out onto the street, but nothing from that world seemed to interest her. I felt she tried to suppress the storm that was slowly growing inside her by closing off any outside stimulation.

She'd always been sensitive to noise and light, but when she was feeling "low," her sensitivity became acute. Everyday sounds, like the bells of the church across the street or a car horn, which the average person wouldn't even notice, could unhinge her. When I sensed she was like this, my whole body would tense; I watched as her muscles tightened and fear gripped her. Sometimes, she'd jump at shadows cast through the living room curtains. "Oh," she'd moan, with her hand to her head, "I feel so terrible. Just terrible."

If Susan and I were lucky enough, we could get Millie to go with us to the public pool in town. But on these rare occasions, she'd have to steel herself against the squeals of children, the lifeguard's shrill whistle, the crowd of people, the "filthy" lawn chairs. Always, there was the feeling that the environment was dirty, unsanitary, loud. As the minutes passed, we became increasingly aware that the situation was overwhelming Millie, threatening her sense of safety and control. Generally, an hour or so was all she could endure.

If I sat down too hard on the couch next to her, she'd react as if the ceiling had fallen in. Sometimes, I'd forget her hypersensitivity; when I did, she might give me a backhand slap, which seemed not so much a punishing blow as a knee-jerk attempt to defend herself.

When Millie was in one of her down periods, she talked often of death. She paced constantly, fussed with the dishes in the sink without really washing them, and got out of bed at four in the afternoon merely to sit down on the couch. "Oh, I feel horrible—just horrible," she'd say, to no one in particular. When Susan and I heard this, we'd think she must be very ill, that perhaps she could die, even if it were from sadness alone.

She'd lie around the house for days in drab clothes—muted earth tones and oversized sweaters. It was as if she were trying to blend in with the furniture, to fade from view. The appearance of a certain nightgown—off-white, flannel, with a faded floral print on it—was a sure sign of coming descent. Often, she'd wear mismatched colors, or pants much too short. If she needed to go out, Susan and I would have to gather the courage to suggest she wear something else.

In Millie's depressed phases, there was little Susan or I could do for her. Engaging her risked stirring up the side of her that was much less manageable than her sadness. Instead, we walked about cautiously and stayed on our best behavior, hoping not to cause her any more upset.

Millie's moods were cyclical, and they often reached a certain crescendo. They began with depression, which almost always led to paranoia and rage. But while she was depressed, she was virtually harmless; this was by far her most common mien during our growing-up years. At the start of a bout of depression, she began chain-smoking, going through a carton of Winstons in a week. When we saw the ashtray filled with cigarette butts, it was time to start tiptoeing through the house.

Then, Susan and I would play quietly in our rooms for hours. I remember hearing the voices of neighborhood kids outside in the evenings and watching them from my window, but I would be too afraid to leave the house, not wanting to incite Millie's deeply suspicious nature. If it became late and we hadn't eaten, I tested Millie's state by flushing the toilet. Susan and I had a silent language, communicating when we were hungry, when we knew we'd have to muster the courage to leave our rooms and get Millie to take care of us. Susan would peer out from behind her bedroom door; I sat for a moment or two, gathering my strength, devising my strategy. I looked through the stair railings, trying to locate Millie before creeping down the stairs. Except for the soft sound of brushing pant legs rubbing against each other and whispers from the TV, the house would be completely silent. I began a slow, soundless descent, ready to turn back if I had to, my stomach churning with fear and hunger.

Susan waited behind her bedroom door as I arranged myself carefully on the couch next to Millie, trying to read her mood. I sat for a while, staring at the television along with her; sometimes, when she needed quiet, the sound would be off. As the sun faded from the night sky, I knew her shows would be coming on soon. I cheerfully whispered to her, "Hey, Mom, it's almost time for the Carol Burnett Show." If Millie cleared her throat, I knew to keep my distance. This nervous tic of hers was, for years, a harbinger of an impending "episode."

It could go either way. She might come back to us; she might not respond at all. As Susan watched quietly and my heart pounded, Millie might crush her cigarette into the ashtray next to her, slowly turning her head slowly toward me as if I'd just uttered something horrible. She'd do so in a way that seemed very labored, as if it hurt to move. "*What . . . did . . . you . . . say?*" she might ask, a long pause between each word, talking through clenched teeth. I'd repeat what I had said, adding that we were hungry.

If she didn't come out of it, Susan and I might try calling our grandmother to bring us something to eat. But Kathryn often baby-sat neighborhood children, sometimes for weeks at a time, and we'd be relegated to stale crackers and butter, or candy I found stashed around the house.

Very rarely, though, Millie might snap out of it suddenly, as if it were all an act. She'd become girlish, even extravagant, telling us it was time to go to the store to pick up a pound of chocolate.

"Let's go, girls!" She was never much of a disciplinarian and, in these times, she'd be even less so, letting us stay up late with her, eating chocolate until we were sick from it.

When she was happy, her happiness spilled over into mania. These were the times when Millie was most compassionate and fun to be around. She'd concern herself with her appearance and dress fashionably. I remember a particular outfit, a fringed leather vest and bellbottom pants, and the mod clothes she wore, all geometric patterns and bright colors. When she tried, she could instantly make herself look stunning.

But those times when she was flying high were also difficult. Another kind of tension created around her happiness: a fleeting but painful sense of fragility. "The great highs were high," Alan once said about Millie, "and the great lows were terribly low." And, of course, when she was feeling good, she'd want Susan and me to be that way, too. No matter what our own moods were, we'd have to rise to the occasion. She might start tickling us to get us to react; sometimes, she'd tickle us to the point of pain. In this way, she was like a child, unaware of her own physical strength; she meant well, but didn't know when to stop. When I got a little older, I learned to kick her off me. "Mom," I'd shout, "stop it!" It wasn't the tickling that bothered me so much as the pain of knowing her buoyant mood wouldn't last. Looking back, I suppose I was learning my own boundaries; I didn't want to continually match my mood to hers.

All too soon, she'd fade from us again, and I'd regret not doing more to keep her happy, not fully enjoying the brief periods of reprieve. Then, Susan and I were back listening to Millie's vague complaints, worrying when she might snap, hearing her say she wished she were dead.

Sometimes we'd even creep into our mother's bedroom like ghosts. We'd stand at the side of her bed, holding our breath, holding still as marble, and check for her heartbeat. "Mom," I'd call out, finally mustering the courage to speak. "Hey, Mom." Susan was always too timid to address her this way. Instead, she'd back away, afraid of waking her if she were, in fact, not dead.

"Mom," I'd say, giving her a little shove. "Hey, Mom. You alive?"

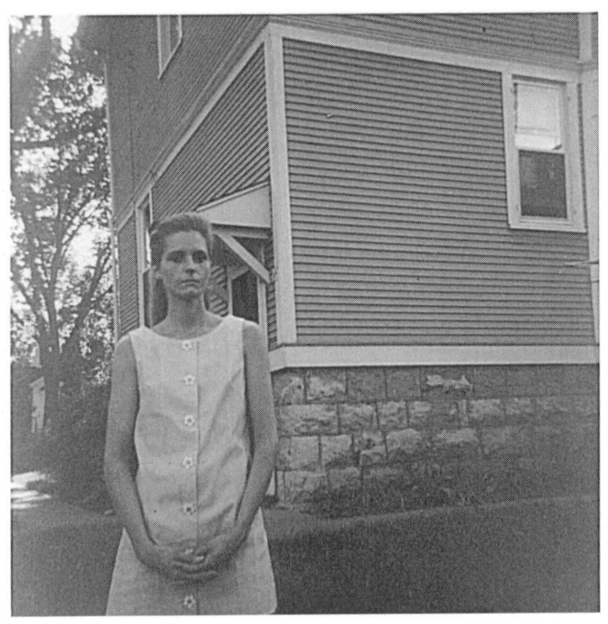

Millie, summer 1970

Chapter Six

They Kept Their Distance

As far back as I can remember, everyone tread softly around Millie, treating her like the proverbial elephant in the living room. Visits to our home, other than by our grandmother, were very infrequent; Millie made it clear she preferred to be left alone. When people were brave enough to come, their stays were often cut short by Millie's constant yawning or obvious indifference. For the most part, her moods remained hidden within the confines of our home, known only to Susan and me.

Kathryn tried, as best she could, to help us. But without confronting the real desperation of our situation or seeing the full picture of our lives, she was applying mere Band-Aids to broken bones. I can only speculate about what Kathryn knew and yet denied about her daughter's illness. Perhaps she thought she was protecting Millie by keeping our struggles secret; perhaps she was afraid that, were Millie's instability to become known, she would lose Susan and me.

For a time, even Kathryn stayed in her car when she came over. She'd wait in the driveway, and we ran out and retrieved whatever she had brought—groceries, or a check to help Millie with the bills.

I don't know why she didn't come in, but I think it was a mixture of embarrassment, fear, and concern that her presence might provoke Millie. She would go months without ever entering our house—never asking about Millie, never suggesting there was anything unusual about the situation.

One day, when Kathryn came to pick up Susan and me, she mustered the courage to come inside. For hours prior, Millie had been on a ranting about things Kathryn had said and done years earlier—not an unusual scene at our house. Kathryn had ruined her life; she had been overbearing, too protective, too involved in her affairs. When Kathryn came through the door, Millie suddenly grabbed her, dragged her inside, and started pummeling her.

As Millie pulled Kathryn to the floor, Susan and I ran to help our grandmother, screaming for Millie to stop. Kathryn tried, for a moment, to reason with our mother. "Not in front of the girls," she urged, but when she realized Millie wasn't listening, she managed to extract herself and run out the door. Susan and I quickly ran after her; clearly shaken, Kathryn fell on her way down the stairs. In that moment, I understood not only the deep embarrassment Kathryn felt, but also her terror of Millie. If Kathryn stayed away before, she had every reason to stay away now, and I began to fear that no one could do anything to help us.

And no one did. The neighbors left us alone; on the few occasions when our father came to visit us, Millie turned him away. Other family members, with the exception of our mother's cousin, Nancy, stayed away completely. No one felt welcome. The tension was palpable whenever our mother would open the door.

While Millie's cousin was teaching near where we lived, she'd sometimes stop by for coffee. During these visits, Millie would laugh and feign cheerfulness; however, as soon as Nancy left, Millie began to get angry. Nancy was boisterous, which seemed to embarrass and even intimidate Millie; she was a large woman.

Millie was careful about her weight and was irritated by people who weren't; weight problems were among the health issues that, in her view, one *could* control, and she resented anyone who appeared not to make that effort. One time, when Millie was sunbathing, a neighbor came over and handed my mother a dandelion puller, noting that it was "good for the waistline." For years, Millie brooded over this comment.

Actually, the only weight problem Millie ever had was being underweight from time to time. "I'm just flat all over," she'd say in disgust on a day when she was feeling particularly dreary. "I don't even have a figure." Though my mother got plenty of admiring looks—from both men and women struck by her beauty—she still thought of herself as not quite fully formed, like an awkward teenager, gangly and undesirable. Once, she even said to Susan, "I can't remember ever looking in the mirror, to this day, thinking I was cute. But everyone around me was always taking pictures."

Nancy and Millie often talked about old times and, for Millie, those memories were often painful. They had spent a lot of time together when they were younger, and sometimes they spoke about experiences on their Aunt Margaret's farm. Millie, a lover of all animals, didn't do well with farming, and these conversations reminded her of images that haunted her.

"Why did I let her in the door?" she said after one visit. She'd have a hard time sitting still afterward; she'd swing her leg furiously on the couch, chain-smoke, pace around the house, and clear her throat more emphatically than before. If she thought of something that really bothered her, she'd direct her anger at Susan and me; she almost always beat us after Nancy's visits. When I asked Nancy, years later, if she had any inkling of what happened to us after she'd leave, she said no. "You were out of sight, out of mind."

Millie's physical abuse waxed and waned during the years of our childhood. I'm still amazed that no one suspected anything. If they did, it was never brought to light, owing to, I believe, their own denial and reluctance to get involved. In kindergarten, I was sent home for coming to school in diapers. A teacher in fourth grade spent half an hour, gingerly combing out the knots in my hair. I have a doctor's note from those early years stating when Susan and I needed to brush our teeth. I also have a get-well card, sent to me by the girl who lived next door at a time when I wasn't sick.

What I found hard to understand was how this girl, with her sweet mother and doting father, could live *right next door* to me. I felt that my proximity to her could make my life somehow less painful. Things on my side of the fence just stayed ugly; nothing made any sense.

Eventually, I began to fantasize about the ways I could die that would be the least painful. I was about ten when I decided to hang myself. I tried to string a rope up on the light fixture in my room. I was standing on a stool, trying to make a knot in the rope, when Millie suddenly opened my door.

"What are you doing?" she asked, seemingly amused. I was surprised and a bit embarrassed and didn't answer her.

She started to laugh. "*You're* not going to die first. I am."

When winter came, Millie would carefully cover all the forced-air heating vents in our house with cheesecloth and masking tape because she believed germs were entering our house through them. She was meticulous about this, using new cheesecloth every year.

One winter when Susan and I were about seven and five, we woke up to a freezing-cold house, so Millie turned up the heat. The house took awhile to get warm, and Susan, who was often afraid to sit next to Millie, positioned herself on the floor, right next to one of the vents, while I sat next to Millie on the couch. I sensed that Millie was at a start of one of her down cycles. She was often irritable and cranky when she got out of bed, especially if it were still morning. But on this particular day, she was already chain-smoking and kicking.

When the heat finally turned on, Susan scooted back toward the vent and brushed up against the cheesecloth, causing a corner to come loose. I noticed right away. Susan tried to lean against it to hold the covering in place, but Millie apparently saw, also, and asked Susan to get another pack of cigarettes from the kitchen. Susan hesitated, and Millie became more forceful. When Susan finally stood up, the cheesecloth fell from the heating vent.

We knew instantly what was going to happen; Millie's body language made it very clear. She stood up, grabbed the rolled-up newspaper by her side, and pushed me out of the way. Then she yanked Susan to her feet by her hair. Susan had looked right at me before Millie grabbed her, as if to say, *Why didn't you get the cigarettes for me?* Millie dragged Susan to the front door, where she put her outside, wearing only her pajamas. Millie told her if she moved, she would kill her. There was frost on the ground. When I turned to look out the window, I could see Susan's breath as she sobbed. She was trying to warm herself, rubbing her hands along her arms, but shivering too much for it to make a difference.

Millie came back inside and locked the door. She sat down on the couch in front of the television, angrily muttering something I couldn't understand, and lit a cigarette.

I knelt over the couch, watching my sister through the picture window in the living room. I started crying but bit my lip; if I showed my fear, Millie might turn on me also. I thought of *The Little Match Girl*, which I had just seen on television. Susan seemed like the orphan made to stand for hours on a stool in the pouring rain. In the show, the orphan died a few days later from influenza. Recalling that, and knowing no one around us cared enough to rescue her, I quickly concluded that Susan could die outside.

Eventually, however, something seemed to shift inside Millie. She slumped back down on the couch, lit another cigarette, and appeared suddenly to come to her senses, looking around as if she'd just woken from a dream. She went to open the door for Susan. "Oh, my darling." Millie cooed, seemingly a different person. I'm so sorry." Susan ran straight to her room and locked the door behind her. Millie was sincere when she apologized, but she wouldn't directly address what she had done. She seemed to lack the ability to understand what had happened.

Later that day, I knocked on Susan's bedroom door, but there was no response.

I didn't know what to do about such incidents. When Millie was abusive, my stomach turned. I became physically sick and terrified, believing Susan was prone to Millie's beatings and mistreatment because she let her fear show.

Sometimes, however, when Millie got to the point of hurting Susan, I'd take action, doing anything to distract her. I'd make up stories, tell her we were being watched, or try desperately to get my mother's attention by insisting someone was coming. I'd open the front door and ring the doorbell several times; usually, by this point, Millie would back off.

One time, Millie pinned Susan to the floor and started to strangle her. I had been sitting on the couch, frozen, watching Susan kick her legs, trying to get Millie off of her. Her face turned red, and she was grasping for Millie's hands. I was sure what I was seeing wasn't real. But when I heard Susan fighting for air, I panicked. I started banging on the window, which looked out to the front yard. Susan managed to escape, run to her bedroom, and slam the door behind her. Millie sat back down on the couch and lit a cigarette, completely disconnected from what had just happened.

The red abrasions were visible on Susan's neck for weeks after that. But no one said a word.

Millie's brother John recalls that it was obvious to him that something bad was going on. He said we'd come to Kathryn's looking ragged and disheveled. He wondered how Susan and I even managed to get to school.

At the time, John was going through a divorce, and he eventually moved back in with Kathryn, whom he relied on despite the tension in their relationship. When Susan and I came to the house,

I got the feeling we were in his territory, that he felt there wasn't enough of Kathryn's goodness to go around. For these reasons, along with his own inability to confront the situation, he stayed out of it. On rare occasions, John would talk with the sheriff next door to us, who he believed was aware of our situation. When I asked what his thoughts were about why no one stepped in to help Susan and me, his response was that the town may not have had a strong social services program.

"If your grandmother hadn't helped," John told me years later, "I think you and Susan might have starved."

The sheriff and his wife, a nurse, were obviously intimidated by Millie, so they kept their distance. Neighbors eventually pulled their children away from me. I was the kid in town who influenced others to do things their parents told them not to do. I had a reputation for being a tomboy, and Millie was no better. I once popped a tire on a neighbor child's bicycle, and the father approached Millie about replacing it. "Absolutely not," she told him, and that was the end of that.

Eventually, I began doing more to get attention. I became a nuisance to the local parish, ringing the church doorbell and then running off. I hid behind trees and parked cars and threw rocks at motorists. I was hardly ever caught.

On any given day, Susan and I could be seen walking around the yard with hardly any clothes on, bruises on our backs and arms. People who knew Millie—her brother John, her cousin Nancy, her mother Kathryn—attributed her anger to the divorce and to the stress of raising two children alone. Over the course of those years, when we lived with Millie on Vine Street, our lives slowly deteriorated but never spilled over enough for the world to see and intervene.

Susan 3, Tina 5 months, Millie 25.
July, 1966

Chapter Seven

The Elusive "Cure"

During the 1960s and 1970s, while Susan and I were growing up with Millie, the field of psychiatry saw an explosion of advances, but none resolved the age-old "nature versus nurture" debate. Thus, theories of etiology and treatment of many mental illnesses, including schizophrenia, spanned a broad spectrum.

Millie's particular background and set of circumstances were consistent with a number of hypotheses. One theory of the cause of mental illness held that parents—particularly mothers—were largely responsible for the psychological health of their children. Kathryn might have exhibited characteristics of the "schizophrenogenic" mother—emotionally cold, distant, and perfectionist. This notion first appeared in the early 1930s, was further developed by psychiatrist Frieda Fromm-Reichmann and was, for decades, considered a possible cause of schizophrenia.

Theories emphasizing the influence of life events and difficulties could also "fit" Millie. She'd experienced the deaths of both her father and stepfather while she was very young, the trauma of boarding school (including the sense of abandonment she must have felt when deposited there), an emotionally charged marriage that ended in divorce, and the ensuing challenges of parenting two young girls by herself. Any one of these could threaten a person's mental stability; from this viewpoint, some degree of disturbance would almost be expected.

Then there was Aunt Libby, who represented a potential genetic predisposition. Though never diagnosed, Libby was clearly paranoid to the point of dysfunction and delusion in her later years.

Had anyone taken the time to weave together the various threads of Millie's life, the evidence of a significant disorder would have been clear. But those threads lay in disarray for years, and connections—typically analyzed within the walls of a therapist's office—were never made. Sometimes I imagined my mother's life like a book, the pages of it scattered, tucked away in drawers, lifted by a gust of wind, and sent to unwelcome doorsteps.

During many years of her life, especially those while Susan and I were growing up, Millie was on a quest for good health, but this always remained just out of her reach. She looked forward to her appointments, to the promise of finding the right drug, the right course of action. But after she had her prescriptions filled, her condition often seemed to worsen. She'd continue taking a previously prescribed medicine along with her new medication or take the new prescription only when she felt like it.

Because Millie had lacked insight into her illness, she often lost sight of the need to take medications (especially major antipsychotics like Haldol or Thorazine) exactly as prescribed; as a result, she suffered the effects of misuse. She'd forget whether she'd take a dose and then take more than the prescribed amount. At other times, she'd go days—even weeks—taking only vitamins, acting on her belief that an ounce of prevention was worth a pound of cure. Not surprisingly, this erratic compliance with her regimen made for very unpredictable behavior.

As a preventive measure, she used to jog, but when she was too far gone, she seemed unable to do anything physical. Her thinking became impaired, so she was unable to recognize when she was losing touch with reality.

Similarly, she was unable to identify things that might help alleviate the tension she felt. On many nights, she was unable to sleep. Often, the leg cramps she experienced—a side effect of Thorazine—were the problem; other times, she'd be wired, as if she'd consumed a lot of coffee or taken a stimulant. Though she often experienced insomnia when she was nearing psychosis, she would stop taking her medication just to get some rest.

As with anyone else, the lack of sleep exacerbated Millie's worries and compounded her hysteria and paranoia, essentially resulting in mania. When she was like this, her eating habits became even less consistent. When she lost her appetite, she also stopped buying us food; when she didn't eat well, her symptoms would worsen.

During her periods of insomnia, she would chain-smoke and roam the house, muttering, restless. She'd yell unintelligibly as she paced her bedroom through the night. I knew Susan, whose bedroom was downstairs, could hear her too. But the next morning, we'd hurry off to school without mention of it, hoping to safely escape even though we knew that we, too, were in danger.

Eventually, after several days, perhaps a week, Millie would become so exhausted that she'd disappear into her room for days.

When she became addicted to the amphetamine high of Dexedrine, she'd counter the effects with Valium or Xanax. Inevitably, her prescription drug use became a vicious cycle of pill-popping, then withdrawal and lethargy, psychosis and, eventually, more drugs. None of her doctors seemed to take into account that she was raising two children alone. Perhaps they never asked; quite possibly, she never told them.

The kitchen cabinet where Millie kept her medications was strictly off limits to us. At any given time, there were about fifteen or twenty prescription bottles inside, along with vitamins, Tylenol, and other over-the-counter pills. Even as a child, I understood that this was the source of a lot of problems for my mother, but I had no power over what went into that cabinet and what was consumed from it. Sometimes she went to it frequently; other times, she wouldn't open it at all.

Whenever Millie left the house (which wasn't very often) when we were young, Susan would go to the cabinet and look at all the pill bottles, counting them, trying to read the labels. The thrill of the forbidden piqued our curiosity. "Don't go in there," I'd warn Susan if I found her snooping; I was terrified that our mother might walk in at any moment. I'd go back and make sure nothing was moved, afraid Millie would find out we'd been peeking. But whether or not Millie could account for all the pills that filled the cabinet, it never appeared to Susan or me that any of them seemed to help her.

During the 1970s, when self-awareness and personal growth became part of the public consciousness, my mother began attending group therapy at Dr. Swanson's home. Though he had been Millie's primary provider of psychiatric care since she was in high school, her faith in him faded as she got older. She began to realize that Dr. Swanson was somewhat unorthodox in his practices and, more importantly, not very helpful. "Nothing happened at the meetings," she said. "He took our money, and I think we all dropped out."

Despite the many medications she took (or didn't take), her running routine, and her vitamins, Millie simply had very little control over her moods. One thing she came to rely on—sometimes to the point of neglecting everything else around her—was television, especially comedies (*I Love Lucy*, *The Tonight Show*, *The Carol Burnett Show*) and Chicago Cubs games. When things were upsetting her, she tried to halt her descents with comedy, with laughter.

Recognizing this, I often tried to step in when it seemed a show was having no effect. I'd start my own comedy routine. And, as if to ensure that she'd be exposed to a steady stream of humor, she bought me joke books, and delighted in hearing me tell jokes. Nothing brought me more pleasure than those times when I got her to laugh. I knew I'd saved her from another hour of misery.

Too often, though, in the heavy tension that preceded an outburst, not even my jokes or her beloved comedies could reach her. She really struggled to lighten up, but it was often impossible for her; I could tell when her laughter was forced, when it was fading. Then, as if she couldn't fight any longer, as if her energy had been completely depleted, Millie would suddenly succumb, snapping like an overstretched rubber band. I believe it took a lot of trust for Millie to laugh with us, to let herself go. She knew she couldn't hold on for very long, and this frustrated her greatly.

She was often deeply affected by what she watched on television (to the extent that Millie's cousin Nancy said that Millie reported having conversations with Johnny Carson). When she'd turn on the news, especially during the Cold War years, she'd be drawn to the tremors about national security and communism, seeming to absorb it all like a sponge. She didn't like to watch the news, but sometimes she did, she said, because she "had to start thinking about sad stuff to stop from laughing."

Millie, of course, had always been prone to extremes, and laughing was one of them. Sometimes, she would laugh uncontrollably and fear that she wouldn't be able to stop. In *Out of the Shadow*, Millie talked about how she eventually had to "give up" comedy. "I was injuring things in my throat," she said. "It was one of those deviated emotions, like crying." The assault of images and noise that the television presented was far too much stimulation for her. So instead, sometimes she'd sit in front of static on the screen, or watch the picture without sound. When I saw these signs, I knew it was only a matter of time until an outburst would occur.

Millie and me (4 years old) 1970

Chapter Eight

An Occasional Mother

When Millie felt good, she'd take Susan and me for hamburgers or ice cream–and actually sit inside the restaurant with us. These infrequent outings gave us a chance to feel like other kids. However, we were always aware that our luck might not hold, that things could turn bad very quickly. Dinner at a restaurant could end with our mother muttering "hurry up" through clenched teeth, shooting panicked glances at other customers. One time, she actually forced us to leave in the middle of dinner, prompting us to ask the waitress to quickly wrap up our food as we hurried to follow our mother back to the car. After that, on the rare occasions when we went to McDonald's or Arby's, we always pulled up to the drive-through window.

I eventually learned to take things one day at a time and to block out the bad times so I could fully enjoy the brief reprieves. These moments and days provided Susan and me with the mother we hung on to and the times that made up for all the rest.

Some nights, Millie might boil a chicken or heat up frozen dinners. We had a gas oven but, once when she was lighting it, flames shot up in her face, burning off her lashes and eyebrows. After that, she was terrified and never used the oven again, so we always ate food that could be served cold or heated on the stovetop.

Because Millie's eating was so sporadic (her medication often blunted her appetite), Susan and I were usually on our own. When Millie did feel like eating, she ate like a child—a piece of Muenster cheese, a jelly sandwich.

Millie tried, with all the strength she could muster, to have normal days. To her, succeeding in this represented a serious accomplishment. Being able to make dinner and do housework like other mothers was a goal she aimed for again and again. The only thing that seemed to ground Millie, to occupy her thoughts for long enough to have good days, was having a clear purpose that was truly important to her.

Millie did work, on occasion, when Susan and I were in elementary school, though these stints never lasted very long. She had a job with the post office, dispatching and sorting mail. She worked as a sales clerk at Jordell's Fine Clothing, a high-end retailer in Hinsdale, where, she told me later, she never should have worked because they paid her three dollars an hour. "There was no reason to work there," she told me, "except for the clothes"—expensive designer clothes, which she spent her paychecks on, then hardly ever wore.

When I asked Millie recently to remind me of some of her other jobs, she recalled a temp agency, a moving company, "warehouses," and "dungeons." Whatever the particular situation was, Millie seemed to derive a sense of usefulness from being employed, which naturally increased her self-esteem. Also, she imagined that Alan could no longer belittle her for her inability to accomplish anything and that Kathryn couldn't harangue her about the lack of structure in her life. She'd prove to them that she could be responsible. Unfortunately, though, Millie's jobs lasted only as long as her moods did, which was never more than a couple of months at most.

When she was out in the world, among people, Millie exposed herself—at least in her mind—to tremendous threat. She'd come home irritable and exhausted. Inevitably, she'd completely withdraw, fail to show up for work or even to call in, and lose her job. In the aftermath, her anger at herself, her confusion, and the lack of support in her life usually led to periods of intense paranoia.

Unsurprisingly, money was always a serious issue for us. Millie received child support from Alan and sporadic paychecks from her jobs, and Kathryn helped out with the mortgage and bills, but there was always a shortage. When Millie would come home with bags of designer clothes and shoes, we had a clue where the money went. However, we weren't resentful; for Susan and me, our mother's happiness was more valuable than money. We always believed we'd be provided for, somehow. Even though our refrigerator and cupboards were often empty and our school clothes too tight, seeing Millie in her new outfits, looking beautiful, gave us hope.

One day, Millie decided to pick up where she had left off so many years before. She'd had enough of part-time jobs; she wanted a career. "I'm going to turn my life around," she announced one bright morning during a rare appearance in the kitchen, where she was making breakfast for Susan and me. So she began taking nursing classes a few nights a week at Lewis University, a midsized school about half an hour from downtown Chicago.

Millie was happier than we'd seen her in a long time. Proudly, Susan and I helped her remember her books and prompted her when it was time to leave for school. We waited up for her to make sure she got home; we assured her she didn't have to worry about us. We were delighted to be trusted, to be given the opportunity to take care of ourselves.

Susan and I were about ten and eight at the time, old enough to stay home by ourselves in the evenings while Millie was at class. Some nights, Kathryn came to bring dinner and check on us.

If our grandmother wasn't coming on a given evening, Susan and I became nearly ecstatic about having the house to ourselves

—free of tension, free from walking on eggshells. We'd play Millie's records, mostly pop vocalists—The Mamas and the Papas, Neil Diamond—dress up in her clothes, and dance through the empty rooms. Home took on a totally different character when our mother was gone. Susan would leave the door to her bedroom open. I'd watch whatever I wanted on television. The house itself seemed to breathe a sigh of relief.

During this time, good things—everlasting stability—seemed possible. Although Millie would still slip in and out of her moods, we had something to work with, concrete reasons for hope. We knew she was trying, and that meant she loved us. *If we could just hold her here …*

For about two years, Millie consistently attended her classes, usually in spurts that would last several months. Not surprisingly, there were occasional nights when she'd have to skip class, too paranoid to leave the house. She even dropped out once but, at the urging of a concerned professor, she went back. Millie was dedicated to being a good student and to proving to everyone—especially herself—that she *could* achieve something worthwhile.

During this fairly long period of stability, Millie was open and engaged in other areas of life as well. She began to date occasionally, able (at least temporarily) to suspend her total ban on men. Millie's behavior around men was complex, almost contradictory at times. She was part femme fatale, part innocent schoolgirl, part terrified divorcée. Her fear likely had its roots in the loss of her father so early in life and Kathryn's refusal to allow her to express any feelings regarding the death of her stepfather. Her stormy relationship with Alan and the trauma of the ensuing divorce kept her, on many occasions, from even setting foot in the same room as a man.

I remember one man, Lloyd, whom Millie met at one of the group therapy sessions at Dr. Swanson's. Lloyd was a divorcé raising three teenage daughters by himself. He was kind, loved by his daughters, and adoring of Millie. Lloyd seemed to have a calming effect on her and, for this reason, he had the extraordinary ability to pass through the impossible boundaries my mother established for men.

Lloyd wasn't unlike our father in some respects; they both were Jewish and were about the same height and had similar features. But in personality, Lloyd was entirely different from Alan. He was warm and compassionate with Millie, and his experience raising three girls seemed to make him a suitable match for our mother, who was much like a young girl at times. Lloyd was unmistakably a father figure—not only for Susan and me but for Millie as well.

When our mother would get ready to go out with Lloyd, Susan and I loved helping her pick out an outfit and watching her dress. She made herself look beautiful, and we were giddily proud of her.

Sadly, though, the demands of adult life—working, relationships, motherhood—began to wear her down. Susan and I could see where things were heading, and we secretly hoped Lloyd would propose. Maybe if they married, our mother would no longer have to work, which would ease the pressure on her.

Millie's training as a nurse required an ability to collect, sort, and interpret data, which she didn't do very well. Such job necessities as taking medical histories and relating information to the attending doctor often overwhelmed her. She'd always had a hard time concentrating, so studying for tests made her despair; often, she failed exams.

Being critiqued by instructors aggravated her mistrust and anxiety, and the day-to-day reality of working in a hospital made her physically sick. She'd come home from school exhausted, complaining about the blood and the body fluids. Worse yet, in choosing nursing, she had put herself into her worst nightmare: She was surrounded by germs.

After school one afternoon, I found Millie in bed. I was confused, because I knew she had class soon. She wasn't looking well–dark circles under her eyes, her hair matted on her pillow.

"I quit," she declared when I warned her that she'd be late.

"I thought you were almost done, though," I said.

"The blood of it," she told me, "just makes me sick."

Eventually, Lloyd did propose to Millie. But soon afterward, he just stopped coming to visit. Susan and I took the end of the relationship pretty hard, but we didn't talk about it, not wanting to upset our mother. Lloyd did well in giving Millie space when she needed to withdraw, and he managed her suspicious temperament for months while dating her. In the end, she slipped into an abysmal paranoia that had her terrified of men again.

"He was such a load," Millie told me. "I felt like I was carrying dead weight with him. Dating is the pits," she said.

Despite Millie's earnest attempts at dating, working, going to school, and mothering, she ultimately would get caught, again and again, in the trap of her own moods. She was simply and utterly at their mercy; so were Susan and I. Yet, if I gave up hope that we could somehow strike the right balance, that we'd get lucky and a good phase might last long enough for our mother to find the right doctor, the right medication, and the right man; finish school; and get a job—or any one of those things—then I would be giving up hope on life itself.

Once, when I was in third grade, I decided to have a friend from school come over for our lunch hour. Susan had done it before, and things seemed to have gone well. For Millie, though, the task was exhausting; it meant waking up before noon to prepare lunch for us and having her mood coincide with the date I chose. There was a lot at stake for me, but I picked a day, and Millie agreed.

The morning of my lunch date, I woke my mother and made sure she remembered our plans. At school, I was so full of excitement and worry that I was barely able to concentrate. I couldn't think about anything except what Millie would make us for lunch. I had told her I wanted the same sandwiches she had made for Susan and her friend the year before.

When the lunch bell rang, my friend and I hurried home. When we turned the corner and my house came into view, panic welled up in me. I was afraid that my mother might still be in bed, that something might have suddenly caused a turn in her mood.

As we got closer, I saw the front door was open, and relief swept over me.

I could hear the hum of the television as we walked through the door. Millie was in the kitchen washing dishes. The house smelled like peanut butter and jelly. *Ha!* I thought. *She did it!*

Millie, as if campaigning for mother-of-the-year, was a vision of perfection, her hair pulled back in a neat ponytail, her skin glowing from suntan lotion and smelling of lemons. She wore yellow rubber gloves and was stacking clean dishes neatly at the side of the sink. She turned to us, smiling grandly, and said, "Afternoon, girls. Lunch is ready." With a sweep of her gloved hand, she motioned for us to seat ourselves at the table.

My friend actually said, "Wow," when she saw the spread of finger sandwiches on a large plate at the center of the table. As if serving us high tea, Millie had prepared four varieties: peanut butter and jelly, bologna, turkey, and cream cheese and jelly. Millie also had hot tomato soup, which she served in bowls alongside little plates for our sandwiches. Glasses of milk appeared along with carefully placed handfuls of potato chips. After we'd stuffed ourselves, she asked us if we wanted more.

I was simply overjoyed.

My friend went back to school that day and told everyone what a great cook my mother was. I was beaming, proud as I could be. Millie had somehow managed to outdo the mothers of the girls I knew.

These were the moments I tried to string together in my mind. I could almost imagine that we were getting there, almost believe we had a chance.

Chapter Nine

Her Ally at What Cost?

Building an alliance with Millie essentially became the primary aim of my childhood. As she descended into psychosis, becoming more suspicious of those around her, isolating herself in her own mind, I tried to follow her into that strange world. I didn't experience the agitation or paranoia that she did, but I could empathize with her feelings—sulking when she was depressed, staying quiet and still when she became terrified of movement.

I believed I had to remain completely in control at all times. To survive in a Millie-centered environment required suppression of my own needs and desires; clearly, she felt threatened by them. So I became compulsive about keeping my mother happy, thinking that if I could control my own behavior and emotions, I could somehow manage hers as well.

Despite my mother's erratic moods, abuse, and hours of ranting, I remained determined to win her love, to be the perfect child for her. I became her shadow, her understudy—not realizing I was emulating a woman who didn't understand her own role. For years, I analyzed Millie, attempting to figure out how to ride her highs and lows, anticipate her needs, and withdraw before she entered the intense psychotic episodes that came with little warning.

Until I was about nine or ten, I actually slept in the same bed with my mother, fearing abandonment; I also believed my constant proximity would ensure that I wouldn't "miss" anything. Even when I wasn't in the same room with her, I was forever aware of where she was, how she was seated and what mood she was in. The strings that tied us together were strong and many.

As I identified with Millie, her feelings often supplanted mine—even when she was paranoid and irrational. When I entered her world, when I agreed that people were watching us or listening to us, I became her ally.

If I asked her what she was feeling and told her I'd help her and take care of her, I thought I had an "in." Every day, I aimed to establish this rapport, to position myself in her good graces. Maybe then, when she felt threats from all directions, I would be exempted from her distrust and fear. If I "protected" her, she might protect me, in return; through this pledge of allegiance to my mother, I tried to cement our bond, to forge a treaty. When she'd get angry with Alan or her mother, I'd commiserate with her, I'd promise her she wasn't alone; no matter what happened, I'd always stick by her.

My loyalty was such that I often defended her irrationally and without question. In the tumult of her psychosis, when she lashed out—at Susan, at Kathryn, at a grocery store clerk who "cheated" her—I'd do the dirty work. I'd irritate Susan in defense of Millie, give Kathryn the cold shoulder—all without knowing whether they'd actually upset my mother. In reality, my actions had little effect, but to me, they were crucial. I could protect Millie from the onset of psychosis, from the people who seemed to diminish her—even from dying from her "illness." Validating her fears became a mission for me, giving me the self-confidence, the purpose I so desperately needed.

But I had little success with this tactic, and the price I paid for taking on Millie's demons was alienation—not only from Susan, Kathryn, and Alan but also from the world at large. The entire construct of my self-esteem and emotional responses became directly linked to my successes and failures in controlling the moods and behavior of my mother.

As a child, I suffered for years from severe leg pain. It felt as if my legs had turned to lead. The pain was so sharp it penetrated deep into my bones. I'd sit with my legs elevated, and my mother would give me Tylenol. This went on about every six months for years. I'd miss things, including school events and outings with our grandmother. I was unable to walk, or even move much.

My mother used to tell me I was having "growing pains." She'd sit at the end of the couch, feeling helpless and sorry for me. She'd smoke and wring her hands, and I'd cry nonstop for hours. The doctors continually told me they couldn't find anything wrong with me. Clearly, they weren't looking in the right places.

Though Susan knew when Millie was disconnecting from us and from her surroundings, she continued to act as if Millie were able to respond appropriately to our needs. As a result, she got caught in the crossfire. Susan did not develop the acute observational skills required to "handle" Millie when she was at the breaking point. Often, because of her relative innocence, lack of strategy, and visible fear of Millie, Susan became our mother's "hostile" target.

I strove to let Susan in on how to ingratiate herself with Millie, how to "stay on her good side" simply by not asking her for anything, but Susan lost interest in trying to heal our mother from whatever ailed her. Susan understood, early on, that taking care of our mother was hopeless—even dangerous—and gave up. When Millie got too weird for her, Susan simply fled. She would go to a friend's house or hide in her room for hours. She'd take off on her bike and visit our grandmother or disappear to our father's house for the weekend.

I understood Susan's need to withdraw, but I still got angry when she left us. *If the three of use could just stick together,* I thought, *we'd be okay.*

For me, the safest place to be was at home. Out in the world, I imagined terrible things could happen; our mother had made that clear. Still, some part of me longed to leave with my sister. For that reason, I spent much of my childhood in awe of Susan. We went home to the same house after school, and we had the same mother and father, yet she excelled in her classes while I was too distracted to concentrate on my studies. She made friends easily; I didn't allow anyone to get close to me. It seemed Susan was developing an escape plan but was keeping me out of it.

I admired Susan's innocence, her refusal to play along with the house's nightmarish code of conduct, her rejection of the irrational and dangerous maze that was Millie's inner world. She lacked either the ability or the desire to appease Millie in the way I did. Susan straightforwardly stated her needs and, in doing so, often caused Millie to become aggravated and anxious. I understood that our mother's love was provided only under certain conditions. I changed myself to suit those conditionals; Susan didn't.

Sometimes, it seemed that, no matter what she did, Susan simply couldn't escape the attacks. Even if Susan hadn't done anything wrong, even if she'd left our mother alone for days, Millie would find a reason to torment Susan.

During Millie's bad periods, we might be playing or watching television; suddenly, our mother would start grilling us about our interactions with other people. If she thought one of us had talked about her, she'd fire questions at us. "What did you say to them at school?" "What did you tell your father?" "What did you tell my mother?" The accusations seemed to come from out of nowhere. But Millie wouldn't back off until she had answers. She wanted to know *which* of us was the traitor. Even when I saw the terror on Susan's face, even if I was the guilty party, I couldn't confess; I'd freeze in the intensity of Millie's interrogation.

Refusing to let Millie down yet intensely scared of her, I resorted to my basic survival instincts—even if this meant incriminating Susan. I was devastated when Susan suffered the consequences. She was being punished for her innocence, honesty, and lack of guile—essentially, for being a child.

Sometimes, I'd try to distract Millie from her accusations by changing the subject, asking her if she were hungry, singing loudly, or tuning in to one of her favorite television shows. But when it was clear to me that Susan was in danger, I might muster the daring to challenge Millie head-on. If she was in my face, asking who I'd been "ratting" to, I'd scream. "You're not the boss of me! I'm not afraid of you!" I tried to overwhelm her and, eventually, she started to fear my strength, my ability to confront her when no one else would. But in the end, I was able to protect only myself; like a predator in the wild, Millie always went after the weaker prey.

When it was too late to divert Millie from an imminent outburst—when she was muttering angrily to herself, twitching, staring at mere static on the television screen—we'd have to quickly plan and escape. The living room, then, would become a lair. Sometimes, Susan and I would go outside rather than risk getting trapped in our rooms, but this would mean somehow traversing Millie's den to reach the front door. Susan did it on tiptoe, holding her breath, meekly moving past Millie. Like a spider attacking a fly snared in its web, Millie might grab Susan and pull her to the ground.

I'd try to pass through as if I were unafraid, skipping by, singing loudly, doing jumping jacks. If I could be louder than Millie was, crazier than she was, I figured I could keep her at bay. If she yelled, I'd yell back; if she told me to shut up, I'd shoot back, "No, you shut up." Sometimes, I'd go right up to her, taunting playfully, "Mom, you wanna fight?" And I could often (though not always) get her to respond positively, even laugh. "Oh, Tina!" she'd say.

When I did succeed, we'd use the seconds when Millie seemed to regain a sense of her surroundings to scramble to our feet and run out the door or race to our rooms. When we would return home or come out of our bedrooms, Millie would be very apologetic. "I'm sorry," she'd say. "I love you. Oh, God, I'm so sorry." Infrequently, she seemed to have the ability to understand what she'd done; these moments of realization nearly destroyed her.

When the storm was over and I'd succeeded in appeasing Millie somewhat, Susan would have already withdrawn. I'd go to her—peek my head into her room, follow her to a friend's house, or ride after her down the street on my bike. "Susan," I'd ask meekly, "are you okay?" But she wouldn't respond. "Want to ride bikes?" Silence. "Susan, can I come in?" I wanted her to forgive my cowardice. I wanted to make it up to her. I couldn't explain what happened to me in those times that I let her down, or why I believed she was more prone to being Millie's victim.

But no matter what I said, how quickly I ran after her, or how I tried to make her laugh, nothing could change the fact of my betrayal. Increasingly, she began avoiding me. "Go away," she'd say, "you've done enough already."

One day, while Susan and I were at school, Millie went out and bought a miniature Bachmann train set. It was quite elaborate—hand decorated with pre-assembled "N" scale buildings, a service station, and a train depot. She told us it was a special treat because she was so happy—rare enough in itself. She moved everything off the white marble coffee table that stood alone in our dining room. It was a room we rarely used, and it felt like quite an event.

The train set was something Susan and I had wanted for a long time, and we were eager for Millie to set it up. That night, we watched our mother open the box, delirious with excitement.

But Millie had something else in mind for the train. It was her treat, not ours. We were not to go near it, let alone touch it.

My sister and I begged her incessantly; finally, Millie agreed to let us operate the train set, but not until she had played with it first. It was fragile and very expensive—so expensive that she made us swear never to tell our grandmother about it. "She'll have a cow," Millie warned us, "and bug me until kingdom come." Susan and I looked at the box cover while Millie read the instructions; it took her a very long time to figure out how to set it up. Susan eventually grew bored and left the room, but I doggedly waited, watching. After a long while, Millie said she needed to go to the store to buy a bridge to connect two pieces of the track. She asked if I wanted to come, but I preferred to stay by the train set.

I listened to Millie's car as it started and made its way down the block. I decided I wanted to surprise her and have the train set up when she got home, but I didn't know how to finish putting it together. So I ran to Susan's room, knowing she could figure it out. Susan was leery; she understood the situation better than I did. But I insisted that our mother would be delighted if we could get the train running before she returned, and she agreed to help.

Susan and I were almost finished when we heard the car pull into the driveway. Suddenly, setting up the train on our own didn't seem like such a good idea after all. We panicked and started frantically pulling the train set apart; as we did, I accidentally broke a piece off the engine. Susan looked stunned for a moment then, instinctively, darted to her room, closing the door behind her. I jumped onto the couch before Millie got inside, and I avoided her gaze as she stood facing me from the dining room, looking down at the empty table. I heard the deep groan she made when she was really angry, and I sensed her coming toward me. "Where's the train?" she yelled. I told her that Kathryn had come by, so we'd had to hide it. This explanation seemed plausible.

Susan must have decided that things were okay because she came out of her room a few moments later, and together we reassembled the set on the table. But when Millie tried to run the train, it didn't move. After some consideration, she realized a piece was missing from the engine. When she asked who had broken the engine, I immediately exclaimed, "I didn't!"

I quickly regretted my cowardly lie. Though I covered my ears with my hands, I heard things crashing to the floor, then Susan's horrifying screams.

Susan back home on a brief visit after moving out, Fall 1977

Chapter Ten

Susan Leaves

Millie's bouts of rage and withdrawal were often triggered by the deep hurt she felt in response to Alan's treatment of her. He refused to consider that what was causing Millie's behavior could be explicable—perhaps even treatable—and not merely a bad disposition or a "bitchy streak." In failing her, he also failed Susan and me.

Being around my father made me feel ashamed of myself; thankfully, we did not get together very often. On the few occasions I did visit him, he made it clear that I was a burden. His rejection and hatred of Millie was not up for debate; defending her would have been like trying to get him to see the value of a termite. He'd scold me in front of his family, declaring that I had poor table manners and bad hygiene ("just like your mother") and made everyone around me miserable. Alan announced that I reminded him of a past that he was deeply ashamed of. Of course, this fed my fears that I would suffer the same fate as Millie, that others saw flaws in me that I couldn't and were simply pointing them out to me. My own worth was directly tied to my mother and to how other people—especially Alan and Nancy, my "other" family—viewed her. I absorbed the feelings of humiliation, shame, and embarrassment; I took their resentment personally.

Susan didn't particularly like going to Alan's house either, but things often appeared easier there, less haphazard and unpredictable. They'd have dinner at regular times; the children were told when to go to bed; the house was well-kept. But when she visited, I imagine Susan must have felt like an intruder, an outsider, an unwelcome guest—just as I did.

Susan's continued relationship with Alan tormented Millie. When Susan would return home after a visit with Alan, she was treated as if she were having an illicit affair. For days afterward, Millie gave Susan the cold shoulder, almost never speaking to her; she studied her with resentful, suspicious eyes. Finally, almost without fail, Millie would fly into a rage. "Living here isn't good enough for you?" she'd shout at Susan. "Then go live with him. Live with him and all his riches," she said, as if she'd suddenly turned into Bette Davis. "He never gave you a dime growing up. He hates you kids."

What Millie feared most about Susan's visits with Alan was that, through Susan, he was somehow able to obtain her private information. I never knew what she feared he'd learn from us, but the only secret we kept from Alan was our mother's repeated crises, and I never thought they were much of a secret to him.

One time, Alan came over to pick up Susan. I was sitting next to Millie on the couch when he rang the back doorbell. Susan had seen his car pull into the driveway and ran to the door, but Millie told her to go back into the living room and stay there. I remember my mother screaming at him, "Get the hell out," but he started pounding on the door, and Susan ran back to it. "Come in," Susan begged. "Hurry!" But Alan eventually left, and Susan was terrified of the consequences of the episode.

When Susan ran out of options, she would call Kathryn. She'd secretly make arrangements to go over, then walk out of the house without a word while Kathryn waited in her car. From the window,

I'd watch them pull away. I wanted to go, too, but I wouldn't ask Millie for a ride. I'd call my grandmother, but she would say that she had already made her trip. "Next time," she'd say. With Susan disappearing more and more, Millie's irrational beliefs and paranoia were mine alone to contend with.

Eventually, as Millie noticed that Susan's escapes were becoming more frequent, she sought to split us, trying to win my affection, possibly hoping I wouldn't try to leave her too. "Your sister thinks she's such a smarty-pants," Millie used to say to me when Susan was in the room. "Doesn't your sister look bony wearing those shorts?" It was as if Millie were daring Susan to leave us; this worried me to no end.

The fact was, I adored my sister. Though I never admitted it then, she was my tether in all those years, the only person I could truly rely on. She provided me with a sense of security I never garnered from Millie. Her ability to distinguish Millie's delusions from reality often saved me from getting lost in the labyrinth of our mother's internal world. But I was continually faced with the choice of abandoning the position I'd gained with Millie to try to "save" Susan. I could never chance having Millie doubt my loyalty; the prospect was just too frightening to me. Needless to say, my relationship with Susan suffered for years to come.

Because I allied myself so closely with Millie, Susan thought I never cared much for her. She felt that Millie and I were a team that left her out and that we'd often gang up on her. She thought Millie and I had a special relationship. We did, but our bond was twisted and inappropriate; I was doing the only thing I knew to get some of my needs met—to survive. Likewise, Susan needed to save herself.

By the time I was nine or ten, my relationship with my sister had seriously deteriorated. On many occasions, I had silently willed Susan to defend herself; fortunately, Susan held on to an integrity that prevented her from becoming enmeshed with Millie the way I was. Little by little, the pressure of our circumstances had consumed us and torn us apart.

One night during the summer before her eighth-grade year, Susan came home around dusk. Millie and I had been watching TV; Susan came in, went straight to her room, and closed the door. Alan's car was still parked out front, and it took me a moment before I noticed he was standing in the entranceway just outside the living room. He hadn't been inside in years; typically, if he were picking up Susan and me, he waited outside in his car. I saw him looking at me from the doorway. For a long time, he stood there, simply observing Millie and me from a distance, but his body language made it clear that something more was going on. He was standing erect, hands in his coat pockets, chest puffed out. Millie didn't turn to look at him until he suddenly stepped into the living room and announced that Susan was moving in with him.

Millie, apparently unfazed, turned back to the TV, but panic swept through me like wildfire. I quickly sat up on the couch, my knees under me. "She's what?" was all I could manage. At once, I felt hurt and helpless on so many levels. I froze. Then I bit down on the back of my hand and began to cry.

I remember the way Alan insisted I stop crying. I was caught off-guard by his tone; he spoke as if he'd been a father to me all along, as if he lived in the house and had authority there. I looked to my mother and hoped, somehow, she'd throw a fit, force Alan to leave and Susan to stay with us. But it was as if she had left the room. I felt like shaking her.

All along, it seemed, her fears had been warranted. She'd always said he'd take Susan from her. In fact, we'd witnessed her paranoia over it every day. But now that the moment she'd dreaded had actually arrived, she simply retreated, disengaging herself.

When Susan came out of her room, she was carrying paper bags containing some of her things. I quickly turned and spoke to her. "Susie, what are you doing?" She wouldn't look at me. She walked behind Alan, looking terribly frightened, urging him to leave. A sweater sleeve hung out from the top of one of her bags.

"I'm moving in with Dad," she said softly, turning to the door.

"Why?" I pleaded. I looked back at Millie. I was desperate. I dug my fingers into the worn fabric of our sofa. "You can't go."

Susan, her brows knitted, seemed about to cry. Alan looked her over to see if she was ready. He put his hand on her shoulder, steering her to the door.

"I don't want to talk about it right now," she said.

I noticed how pale she looked, how completely exhausted she seemed. She'd always been terrified that our mother would try to kill her if she left.

When Susan reached the door, something suddenly sprang up in Millie, rousing her from her passive silence. Alan had always been terribly intimidating to her, but now that he was about to leave, she mustered the courage to react. Millie slowly turned to Susan, leaning forward. In her most honeyed voice, as if Susan were a very small child who had lost her way, she said, "Susan, sweetheart, you don't have to do this."

I remember the look on Susan's face, the way she turned her head away, as if she'd been slapped. Millie started to speak, but Alan cut her off by saying, "You have a problem with it, you can contact my lawyer," he said. With that, they left.

For hours afterward, I sobbed uncontrollably. Millie paced around the house, returning occasionally to the couch, where I was sitting, to light a cigarette. Then she'd get up, walk to Susan's room, peer in, and wring her hands.

The leaves on the trees lining Vine Street had just begun to change. It was already beginning to feel cool, which meant fall would come early that year, bringing with it the promise of a long, cold Illinois winter. For a long time, I stared out the window, feeling sick to my stomach, half expecting Susan to come walking up the street. Nothing looked the same.

How could Millie have just let her go like that? It took me years to realize that she had no choice. She was the weaker one, unable to defend herself, let alone her daughter. And Susan had clearly made her choice.

Millie tried to console me that night, and she did so in a way that suggested she'd managed to distance herself from the situation, almost as if Susan were no longer her daughter. "You poor thing," she said to me, stroking my hair with her hand. "How could she just go off and do this to you?"

I didn't answer. I think Millie must have been as shocked as I was, but in my grief, I hardly noticed.

In the days and weeks after Susan moved out, I seemed to lose the ability to cry. I tried to do everything Susan had taught me—making sure the time was accurate by looking at more than one clock in the house, always preparing something to eat for breakfast. But I dreaded walking out the door and leaving my mother. Sometimes, on the way to school, I looked down to make sure I wasn't still wearing my pajamas.

I thought of all the times I hadn't protected Susan from Millie's anger, the times I had let her take the blame for something I'd done. I'd been mean to her—horrible even. I was a wretched sister, always siding with our mother, never standing up for Susan. I went over everything I could have done differently. I'd created my own mess. I'd made Susan leave.

As Millie sank deeper into depression, I blamed myself. She had already been sick and in pain, and now I had caused her more grief. Locked into my own despair, I was unable to reach her.

After a few long months had passed, I asked Millie if we could get a dog. She'd always rejected my request in previous years, but this time—wishing for the added companionship herself—she agreed. She began looking in the newspaper and making a few calls and, after a couple of nights, we were on our way to pick out a puppy from a Maltese litter. Millie fell in love with the little dog we chose and named him Winston—after her brand of cigarettes.

Wherever Millie went, Winston was always right there at her

feet. He slept in bed with her and went with her to the store. Often, I'd come home from school to find Millie in her usual place—on the couch, watching TV, chain-smoking, one of her crossed legs swinging nervously—with Winston right by her side.

A few times, when I came home from school and Millie was just getting out of bed, she'd make something to eat for herself—and for Winston. She'd cut up bits of steak and potatoes, feeding the dog with the same fork she'd use herself. Then she would give me a frozen TV dinner. I felt as if I were a friend who had fallen from favor and been replaced by someone new.

When I was a child, one of my most precious possessions was a dollhouse that was handed down to me by my mother. She loved that dollhouse and, when she was feeling up to it, she took great care in decorating it with tiny pictures on the walks, wallpaper and miniscule kitchen utensils. It was remarkable how much she enjoyed arranging everything, fixing it just right. No Kathryns, no Alans, no children in that little house made demands on her or judged her.

I hardly ever played with the house myself, fearing that it was far too fragile for my hands. But I loved it all the same, and we kept it in the living room on the hearth. One day, upon returning from school, I noticed that Winston had taken one of the figures—the mother in her brown woolen dress—along with some furniture and was chewing them as he sat next to Millie on the couch. She either didn't notice or didn't care.

I suddenly lost control. For months, everything had been building up in me—Susan's leaving, Millie's withdrawal, my own depression. I'd had enough of the dog never leaving Millie's side, stealing my mother like a competitive sibling.

At last my loneliness and anger erupted. I lunged at Winston and pushed him off the couch. It was more for effect than anything else, but Millie, only slightly jarred by my outburst, turned to me and said, flatly, "Don't hurt the dog."

After Susan moved out, our house became filthy, and there were rarely any groceries. On occasion, Kathryn came to bring food and to help clean up after the dog. But she had been spending more and more time away, sometimes weeks on end, babysitting children whose parents were on vacation.

When I needed to get out of the house—to get away from Millie, the dog, and the ache of Susan's absence—I headed over to Kathryn's on my bike. Sometimes, I'd show up at her house and, if she wasn't home, John would answer the door. He'd shrug when I asked where Kathryn was. I sensed he knew but didn't want to tell me. He simply didn't want to get involved. Perhaps, I thought, Kathryn had taken these jobs not only to help us with our bills but also to get away from me.

One time, I managed to track her down. She looked bothered and didn't want to let me inside. "I'm working," she told me. "Get on home."

When my sister left, Millie's decline seemed to gain momentum. Eventually, she talked less about Susan, and her behavior became increasingly bizarre. Some days, she'd decide to wear makeup for no apparent reason, but she would apply it oddly, the eyeliners veering off the natural curve of her eyelid. She wore pants that were far too short (even if short was than fashionable), and she'd choose combinations that didn't match. Her hair, which she didn't seem to wash any longer, became tangled and stringy, and there seemed to be a gauntness about her that gave her the appearance of someone impoverished and lost. When I did mention Susan, whatever the context, she simply brushed me off, saying, "I don't want to talk about it."

She'd sleep continually, sometimes not leaving her bed for days. When she did make her way to the kitchen to get something to eat, she still looked exhausted. Her pale nightgown hung off her. She was thin, ghostlike, her face sunken and hollow. Sometimes, I couldn't even look straight at her; it was too much for me to bear. Once, I tried to break the tension by asking her if she were feeling sick.

"I always feel sick," she replied. "I've had a stomach ache for ten years."

Her periods of paranoia seemed to lessen as the depression consumed her, though her anger was still as fiery as ever. If she came after me for not cleaning up Winston's mess (which she didn't like to do herself), I'd run out the door, take off on my bike, and ride around until well after dark. When I returned, I'd hide outside the house, waiting for her to go to bed so I could sneak back inside.

Eventually, though, Millie seemed too worn down to come after me. Some days, she could barely move from the couch, and it seemed as if all her energy went toward her desire to disappear.

I started doing things I thought might have an effect on her—any effect. I'd choose a record from her collection and play the same song over and over, as loud as the hi-fi could play it. Sometimes, when this got her attention, she'd come after me with a belt. Pain was real, acute, concrete; with its presence, we both became solid human beings once again for a moment, not intangible ghosts stuck in the past. I felt real anger and even allowed myself to detest her. However, the price of inciting these responses from her was high.

One night, as Millie sat beside me on the couch, I called Alan's house and managed to get Susan on the telephone. I begged her to come back. "Please come home," I pleaded. "I love you." Millie got up and began to pace. When I was crying too much to talk anymore, Millie took the receiver from me. "You broke her heart," she said, but Susan had already hung up.

I rested my head on my mother's lap, sobbing but comforted by the sway of her leg, the smell of her cigarettes, the buzz of the Cubs game on TV. She stroked my hair, saying dreamily, repeatedly, "How could she do this to you?" and letting me know Alan didn't quite love me. (In other words, I shouldn't get any ideas about going to live with him.) "He doesn't want another girl," she'd say. "He got what he wanted. He won't be calling anymore." There was always this thorniness about my mother's attempts at comforting me, as if something in her couldn't truly feel, let alone express, anything other than pain. In a trance-like monotone, she'd tell me, "We're a team now. All we have is each other."

As Millie got out of bed less and less often, our house became a disaster. She would spread newspapers on the kitchen floor because she couldn't stay out of bed long enough to take care of Winston. The papers became so drenched in the dog's urine and feces that our entire house began to reek. At first, I circumvented just those parts of the kitchen. Then, I avoided going into the kitchen altogether, hoping she'd wake up and clean up the mess but, when she did rise, she simply took what she needed from the refrigerator, made herself a cup of coffee, and walked back out. If I got really hungry and absolutely had to go into the kitchen, I'd hold my breath. Finally, I'd give in and clean up after the dog, angry that I was the one looking after him.

Soon, I grew as depressed as Millie, and it began to seem as if the house wasn't big enough to contain such despair. Unlike her, I had to get out of bed early every morning, go to school, and face the world. That was enough to deal with. I waited for Susan to come back, but she never did; I knew Millie wasn't going to do anything to bring about her return. It seemed she'd just let Susan go, and I began to resent her passivity.

I imagined showing up at Alan's, crawling in through a window; finding Susan crying, unwanted, and alone; and taking her back home with me. At least with her in the house, life wouldn't feel quite as bleak. My plan wasn't realistic, however, because I didn't even know the way to my father's house.

As Millie's depression grew more severe, she talked with increasing frequency about killing herself. She wandered around the house in that thin, pale nightgown, muttering, "I just feel like dying." When I heard this, it seemed like the world was coming to an end. I became utterly preoccupied with her health, worrying that she might not be alive when I came home from school.

1978

Chapter Eleven

My Escape

One cold and rainy night about two years after Susan moved out, my mother and I were watching television. She was sitting on the floor doing exercises, her legs stretched out in front of her. *Little House on the Prairie,* a show I adored, was on, but Millie wanted to watch a late-night baseball game.

We began fighting about it, shouting back and forth. "You always watch what you want to watch," she said, as if we were now sibling rivals. I stood my ground, and she hers.

Finally, with disgust, I changed the channel but, by that time, Millie had left the room. She pulled out a sweatshirt and said she was going for a run. It surprised me, since Millie never ran when it was raining.

Before she left, she said, "I want you out of my life for good." She then went on to blame me for her many problems and to talk about how much happier she would be without me.

"I hate you," she said, heading out the door.

Though I'd heard these things before, those words, coming from my mother's mouth at that moment, stung me deeply.

It was late October, and it had just begun to get dark earlier. The moon was high between clouds, and the air smelled of wet leaves. Already, the temperature had started to fall. It was past eight in the evening; most of the nearby homes were illuminated only by the flickering glow of a TV screen. A neighborhood dog barked, and I realized how quiet the house had become, even as Millie's words resounded in her absence.

I rose from the couch and suddenly felt a strange sense of lightness and relief. I went into the kitchen, where I began cleaning up Winston's dirty newspapers. The voice in my head, which usually narrated my every move and struggled to make sense of things, fell silent. After laying fresh newspaper on the floor, I opened the cabinet where Millie kept all her medications. There were about fifteen different bottles; I removed several of them, leaving Tylenol and aspirin in the cabinet. I shook out bunches of pills from several bottles—about ten from each—leaving enough so that Millie wouldn't notice anything unusual. Colorful pills dropped to the floor where I stood barefoot. I shoved handfuls into my mouth and held them there. The coatings had melted a bit, leaving red and yellow splotches on my hand, which I cupped to bring water to my mouth.

My heart was thumping; it pounded in my ears. I heard the sound of my own breath. I felt somehow as if I were outside my body. I gripped the kitchen counter to steady myself.

I heard the front door open and close; Millie had returned. I still had a couple of medication bottles open on the kitchen counter. I quickly snatched the bottles, grabbed the scattered pills with my other hand, and ran into the bathroom, shutting the door behind me. When I started dumping the pills into the toilet, I heard my mother calling my name.

Millie heard me crying through the bathroom door and asked if I was all right. "Leave me alone!" I shouted. She started to open the door, but I slammed it on her hand. Her anger, kindled earlier that night, rose in her again. I didn't have the energy or strength to fight her off; she overpowered me, forcing the door open. The pills were still floating in the toilet.

"What did you do?" she barked.

I told her I had flushed her pills because I was angry with her. "Do you know," she thundered, "how expensive those are?" The bathroom was very small and left no room for me to dodge Millie's flailing arms. She grabbed my hair and pushed me against the wall; I slipped, and my head hit the toilet. Millie was now wild with rage, and there was no calming her, no chance for talk. She dragged me by my hair along the floor, out into the kitchen. I imagined dying at my mother's hands. I begged her to let me go, but I doubt she even heard me.

I couldn't fight back. My arms and legs began to feel heavy, and my vision went blurry. For some reason, she eventually stopped beating me and left me alone; perhaps she sensed the energy leaving my body. Realizing I might not have much time, I began to panic. I reached for the telephone beside me and called Kathryn. "I need you to come get me right now," I said. "Hurry."

As I hung up, I saw Millie, sitting on the couch with a cigarette, staring vacantly at the TV.

I threw open the front door and sat on the steps. Our disagreement had clearly been loud enough to draw the neighbors' attention. I could hear voices as people came out onto porches, but I couldn't make anything out and didn't care to. My senses dull, my thinking slow, I lay my head on my knees, hoping I could stay awake.

At last, Kathryn's car pulled up. I got to my feet and started down the front walk very carefully, one foot in front of the other, sensing many eyes following me.

It was dark inside the car, and I don't think Kathryn saw my matted hair, cut lip, and tears. "Please just get there," I begged, afraid I might pass out on the way. She wanted to know what had happened, but I told her not to ask any questions. When she insisted, I said, mostly to quiet her, "She's been hitting me."

I warned Kathryn to leave me alone; she understood what I meant. When we walked into the house, John was sitting in his chair, watching TV as usual. He looked away when I walked past him.

Upstairs, I quietly closed the door behind me and collapsed on my grandmother's bed. My head was spinning, and I was slowly losing feeling in my arms and legs. A photo of my sister and me, when we were younger, sat on the nightstand next to the telephone. Susan and I were embracing each other so enthusiastically it looked as if we might have toppled over after the picture had been taken.

There was a knock at the door; Kathryn came in before I could say anything. "Please go," I begged her. I knew she wasn't sure what to do. Calling the police or the hospital wasn't something she'd feel comfortable doing, so she asked if I needed anything. When she left the room, I reached for the telephone and dialed Alan's number. I wanted—needed—to talk to Susan. Nancy picked up, and I had to struggle to get my mouth to form words. She handed the receiver to Susan; my sister knew immediately that something was very wrong. She asked if I was going to be okay. "I don't think so," I whispered. When she pressed for more, I admitted I had taken some of Millie's pills. What she said next wasn't clear. I lost consciousness.

When Susan and Alan showed up at Kathryn's door, John refused to let them in. Susan begged desperately, saying I was in trouble, but John shouted back at her, insisting I was fine. He threatened to call the police if Alan so much as set foot in the house. Susan told Alan to wait outside, then ran upstairs, past John and Kathryn, to find me lying motionless on Kathryn's bed.

I vaguely remember Susan's attempts to rouse me. She managed to get me to my feet by putting her arms beneath mine and lifting me. My knees buckled; she did her best to carry me. By the time she got me down the steps, she had to drag me to the front door. Kathryn and John stood by and watched. Finally, outside, Alan picked me up, put me over his shoulder, and carried me to his car.

Chapter Twelve

Someone to Watch Over Me

Alan and Susan took me to Hinsdale Hospital. The ER physician who examined me discovered abrasions on my neck and back and a small laceration on my lip. Hearing of my ingestion of drugs, he called Millie for details. She explained that we had had an argument earlier that night, after which she had gone for a run. When she returned, she said, she found me incoherent and unsteady, then discovered that I had taken some of her tetracycline and Fiorinal pills. She immediately called the police to take me to the hospital. According to the medical records, Millie assured the doctor that she kept her medications in a locked cabinet and that she wore the only key around her neck at all times.

After a while, the attending physician returned to the waiting area to update my family on my condition and treatment plan. He said that I'd remain on the pediatric floor while they got the various medications out of my body and stabilized me. Then, after an evaluation, I'd be transferred to the psychiatric unit. He told them that I was receiving only intravenous hydration and charcoal to induce vomiting and assured them that I would be fine. I spent the rest of the evening drifting in and out of consciousness. Various faces appeared above me from time to time; cries from other patients occasionally interrupted my sleep. For long periods, I forgot what had happened and where I was.

The following day, before I was transferred, my father visited me in the pediatric ward. My wrists were secured to the bed; I had repeatedly pulled out my intravenous tube. When Alan walked in, the nurse asked that he not stay long. She explained that I'd been having a "bad morning" (somewhat euphemistically, inasmuch as I'd punched a nurse and broken her glasses) and that I was still groggy from the tranquilizer they had administered to help me rest.

My father walked slowly to my bedside. As I peered out from beneath my sheets, my eyes met his. He said, "Baby . . . why?"

Later that day, as I was wheeled up to the psychiatric ward, I opened my eyes and watched the ceiling lights. They passed above me, one by one, like the dotted lines of a highway.

I was frightened by having survived my suicide attempt. Now, I was trapped in a hellish limbo, a sort of half-life. I wanted Millie near me, yet I didn't want to go back to how things had been. The house on Vine Street had become a prison for us; in Susan's absence, my world had gone from bad to worse. However, I didn't want to be in the hospital, either. I didn't belong anywhere.

The window in my new room let in very little light, and the only view was of a parking lot. I could hear the frenzied activity of the hospital rushing by my door, but it seemed very distant to me, as if I were under water, sensing movement and light coming from above the surface. Late the next day, as the sun sank behind the trees, Millie, Susan, Alan, and Nancy sat together—a very rare occurrence indeed—with my doctor, Dr. Swanson, who had been Millie's psychiatrist for some years. The meeting had been organized to gather some family history and to try to determine why I'd attempted to take my life.

Susan recalls that she sat next to Alan, her arms wrapped around her middle. Nancy was on Alan's other side. Susan recounts the events of the night of my suicide attempt. She said that when she and Alan arrived at Kathryn's, my uncle John wouldn't open the door. "He hated my father so much, he wouldn't let me in," she said. "Dad was right there standing next to me, and my uncle kept saying, 'your Goddamned father.' I told him my father could wait outside and that I just needed to get Tina." She paused and began to cry.

"Meanwhile, my sister was dying upstairs in the bedroom," she sobbed.

Susan turned to Millie, who was fidgeting nervously, crossing and uncrossing her legs. Her expression showed that she was present against her will. "He wouldn't let me in the house," Susan continued. "He barred the door, and I had to push my way past him. Grams was inside, but she just stood there."

Millie, growing more uncomfortable by the minute, gripped the arms of her chair and began to swing her leg. She had always hated hospitals, and being with both Alan and the psychiatrist didn't help matters any. She probably worried that she, herself, might be involuntarily committed.

"Maybe he was just trying to help," Millie suggested, referring to John.

"No, he wasn't," Susan asserted. "No one was. My sister was passed out on the bed, and I had to drag her down the steps and try to haul her on my back."

Millie sat up in her chair, leaned toward Susan, and addressed her directly. "Your grandmother would have taken care of her, Susan. There was no need to—"

Alan cut her off and spoke with force. "Take care of her?"

"John was just protecting Tina," Millie told Alan, sharply, uncrossing her legs.

Alan began again, but Dr. Swanson intervened. "Please," he said, and everyone fell silent. He reminded them that this meeting's purpose was to discuss the reason for my hospitalization.

"Alan," the doctor then asked pointedly, "could you give me an idea why you think your daughter tried to kill herself?"

According to the medical records, Alan explained to the doctor that Millie had "psychiatric problems" and depended on me greatly. He claimed there had been a "reversal of roles" that was negatively impacting my growth and development and made my living with Millie unhealthy. "Nevertheless," the meeting report concludes, "he did agree to Tina's going home with her mother . . ."

When I had the vision, I had been lying in my hospital bed with my eyes closed. I had already begun to memorize my surroundings—the crack in one of the ceiling tiles by the window, the faded geometric pattern of the blanket on my bed, the vase of wilted flowers next to my bed. I opened my eyes again, and hints of light passed through the metal screen that covered the small window to my right, illuminating bits of dust floating in the room. As the sun began to set that night, I drifted, hoping I wouldn't survive these days, praying to God to *uncreate* me. I tried in vain to avoid any thoughts of what lay ahead if I survived just one more day.

"Christine," I heard someone say suddenly. No one except Alan, when he was being stern, ever called me by that name. I opened my eyes and propped myself up on my elbows. A light filled my room, blinding me. It seemed to radiate warmth, like strong sunlight. At first I didn't see anyone, but I strongly sensed a presence. I thought for a moment, trying to recall whether it was morning and how long I had slept.

Eventually, a man appeared. He was draped in a white robe, a soft halo of light surrounding his head. He looked like I imagined God did. He came and stood at the foot of my bed. "I'm sleeping," I whispered, uncertain of what I was saying and to whom I was speaking. When the words came out of my mouth, I realized I actually wasn't asleep.

The man extended his hands to me, and I was not afraid, though I didn't understand who he was or the reason for his presence. Instead, I felt embraced by a powerful and unexpected warmth and lightness.

"I love you," he said to me.

"Tina," I heard the nurse say firmly. She was beside my bed trying to rouse me. I tried to summon the image I had seen, as if attempting to resume a dream that had dissipated upon waking. After she spoke again—"Tina?"—I sat up, grabbed the vase of flowers next to my bed, and threw them at her, narrowly missing her head.

I wondered if I had become like the other patients in the psych ward at Hinsdale—muttering, hallucinating, exploding in sudden rage. I never told anyone of the vision and never tried to determine whether it was real, but I had the inexplicable sense that someone was watching over me—that regardless of all the crap I had done, someone loved me. For weeks after, I meditated on those words, wrapped myself in them: *"I love you."*

"Oh, sweetheart," Millie said to me, caressing my hand. She'd been coming every day, oddly dressed and disheveled, looking as if she'd not slept in days. "I'm so sorry they did this to you." I'd been in the psychiatric ward less than a week, but Millie was urging me to come home. She took hold of my shoulder and tried to get me to sit up. "You need to get up and walk around to show them you're okay." She turned my legs to the side of the bed. "C'mon, I'll help you," she said. "The stronger you get, the sooner we can get you out of here."

I was too weak to sit up. The air felt heavy and thick, as if an invisible force hindered my movements. My mind no longer seemed able to govern my body.

"She's your baby," a male voice announced. I looked toward the source of the sound and saw an old man standing in the doorway of my room.

Turning angrily toward the door, Millie said through gritted teeth, "Get out of here, you stinking, dirty old man."

"I just wanted to see your baby," the man explained softly.

"I said get out of here!"

Millie stood up, but the floor nurse, who had heard Millie, walked up beside the old man and took hold of his shoulders. She spoke softly to the man, then gently steered him away from my room.

Rapidly redirecting her fury, Millie glared at the nurse and demanded, "Why did you do this to her? She needs to keep moving. You can't keep her confined to a bed."

Noting Millie's hostility, the nurse started to reply cheerily, but Millie cut her off. "Her bed is all wet. You didn't even get her to the bathroom!"

The following morning, as the charge nurse busied herself dispensing medication to patients, the old man shuffled his way back into my room. I could hear him approaching, so I rolled over, peering up at him from beneath my sheets.

"I'm not going to hurt you," he said. Appearing to be in his mid-seventies, he reminded me a little of Jack Lemmon in his later years, with gray hair and a sweet, grandfatherly face. "You're too young to be in here. You're just a little baby," he cooed.

The nurse stormed in, ordering the man to leave. He seemed hurt but complied. A few moments later, I heard a voice in the hall.

"Hey, old man. Ain't you dead yet?"

The next afternoon, Millie was back at my side, doting on me, complaining to the nurse about everything under the sun. "You don't know anything about medicine," she declared. "She needs sunshine and fresh air, not some stuffy hospital room."

When the nurse walked in with a pill for me to take, Millie nearly knocked the cup of water from her hand.

"Get out of here," she growled at the nurse. "The drugs are making her spacey."

The nurse explained that the pill was just a vitamin, but Millie would have none of it. "You're all alike," she snapped. The nurse winced, spilling a few drops of water at my side. "Every one of you,"

Millie continued with unmistakable contempt. "If everyone took these drugs, we'd all be in this godforsaken place."

Whenever Millie started using words like "godforsaken," when she started pausing between words, I knew she was nearing the limits of her control.

However, for the first time, I didn't flinch, even though I recognized her state; I didn't react at all. It was as if I were watching a total stranger, perhaps a woman who'd wandered into my room. Although frightened that she might hurt the nurse, I sat back and relished the luxury of not having to intervene. In that moment, sitting in a torn leather chair at my bedside, Millie looked small and wizened. Her cheeks appeared more angular and sunken and her words less threatening than usual, as if their usual voltage had been drained. I studied her face as she seethed.

"There's no need to get excited," the nurse said, trying to mollify Millie. She pointed out that I hadn't eaten for several days and that the doctor wanted to ensure that my immune system didn't weaken.

"You wouldn't want your daughter to get a cold or the flu while she's in here, would you?" she asked, evidently hoping to appeal to Millie's maternal instinct.

Millie looked exasperated, and the nurse handed me the pill.

"Don't worry," Millie said conspiratorially after the nurse left the room, "I'll get you out of here."

Years later, I realized that that day was one of the first times in my life when I experienced a kind of immunity from Millie. My place in the hospital kept me safely removed from her, but it was more than that. I was able to gain a perspective I never had in my everyday life, which included precious little input from the outside world. Though I didn't doubt Millie's concern for my well-being, she rarely expressed positive regard for me, and I always received it with suspicion. Millie, I suddenly saw, was in a panic during my hospital stay. Just as Susan was my compass, I was Millie's. I knew that in attempting to take my own life, I'd committed an act of vengeance against Millie.

Dr. Swanson noted a decline in my spirit following one of Millie's visits. He wrote in my chart:

> *Tina changed quickly from a negative, silent young adolescent to behaving more like a 3- to 5-year-old demanding and frightened little girl. She cried frequently for her mother, and early when her mother would visit, she would cling to her and make every effort to get her mother to take her home.*

After this, Millie was not allowed to visit me until the last day of my stay, when Dr. Swanson called another family meeting. This time, only Alan and Millie attended.

At Dr. Swanson's request, I brought a written list of issues I felt I needed to address with my mother and father. When a nurse escorted me into the room where my parents and doctor were waiting, a shiver of dread ran through me.

They were sitting in an odd arrangement. Millie and Alan were across from each other, and Dr. Swanson was between them. As I walked in, Alan offered his hand to me. The gesture confused me. "Come here, darling," he said.

Had he been on stage, playing the part of an affectionate, concerned father, he would undoubtedly have been quite convincing. I, however, was a somewhat tougher audience.

I sat down next to Alan, and he held my hand. Despite my misgivings, I assumed my role as the cared-for daughter.

When the doctor gave me a nod, I pulled my crumpled list from the pocket of my hospital gown.

"I have a list of things." My words were tinny and seemed to fall on deaf ears.

"Go ahead," the doctor encouraged, loudly, as if demonstrating to my parents what was required of them.

I let go of Alan's hand and looked at him. My throat seemed to close suddenly. When had I ever addressed him this way? When had I communicated to him any of what I had lived through since his departure over a decade ago? I sat for a moment, unable to move or speak. When the words finally came, it seemed to me as if someone else were speaking.

"Why," I sputtered, "why did you call me foolish on the phone a couple nights ago?"

"Don't you think this was a foolish thing to do?" he replied.

I looked at the doctor, but he, too, looked a bit uneasy. Millie, on the other hand, looked much as she always did—motionless, vacant.

With a surge of fortitude that surprised even me, I patiently reminded my father of the terrible things he had said to me about Millie through the years. Engaging Millie, at this point, seemed to me the right thing to do.

Dr. Swanson broke in. "Tina, is there something you'd like to say to your mother?"

I bit my lower lip and looked at her. I imagined my mother as a girl my age, feeling lost, abandoned, resigned to recede from a world that was uninterested in her plight. For the first time, I wondered what she had hoped for when she was my age, whether she had ever imagined a life that resembled the one she was living.

I softened when I spoke to her. I simply requested that she pay more attention when I was talking, that she at least try to act as if she cared.

My mother's eyes filled with sorrow as she looked back at me. I felt as if I had scolded a young girl for something beyond her understanding.

Suddenly, as if to punctuate what I considered a futile meeting, a nurse interrupted us, informing the doctor that a Department of Child and Family Services (DCFS) representative had arrived to meet with us.

Upon arrival at the hospital, as a result of my attempted suicide and minor bodily injury, the ER physician requested a review by DCFS. Terrified of incriminating Millie or providing a reason for a longer hospital stay, I denied to the DCFS caseworker that Millie had ever abused me. She reported that she found no conclusive evidence of child abuse, and Dr. Swanson decided that no further action was necessary.

Once again, a nurse barged in—this time to alert the doctor of a patient in crisis. Quickly, he apologized and asked Alan and Millie to follow him; he needed their signatures on my discharge papers.

The nurse led me back to my room, and I changed into my own clothes. After I had dressed, the nurse returned to wish me luck. Quite to my surprise, she added, "I hope you realize that your father really is a good person. He just wants what's best for you."

"I know," I said politely, tacking on a weak grin.

She stood up and gave me a hug, and I watched her walk out the door. After she had gone some way down the hall, I flipped her my middle finger.

The elevator couldn't descend fast enough for me. I pressed the ground floor button repeatedly while my parents stood behind me in silence. As we stepped out, Alan, in his new, stilted tone, asked, "Well, darling, how does it feel to be out of that place?"

"I'm not out yet," I replied. "But when I am, I'll tell you."

On my discharge papers, Dr. Swanson recommended that Millie return once a week and that my entire family meet with him monthly. However, no follow-up sessions were ever held.

Chapter Thirteen

Who Will Take Me In?

Following my suicide attempt, my father filed for custody. Whether or not this is what he really wanted, I never knew, but it was no longer a secret that Millie's parenting was not conducive to my well-being. We were given a court date of November 1, 1979.

I had been discharged from Hinsdale Hospital on Halloween, two weeks after I had been rushed to the emergency room. As Millie drove me back home, dusk was settling. I looked out of the car window, watching children run from door to door, giddily climbing steps, tripping on their costumes. "Oh, look at that one," my mother said, her eye on the road. I couldn't manage small talk. My arms felt leaden, and the world outside the car—the crisp air, the crunching leaves beneath the feet of the ghosts and goblins, the nearly full moon—felt hopelessly unreachable. It was as if I were watching a film of someone else's life.

When we reached the house, it seemed small and unfamiliar. In the first sharp pang of feeling I'd had in weeks, I realized that I no longer wished to be a prisoner in the house on Vine Street. Yet, equally unsettling, I didn't want to be anywhere else. Perhaps I *was* better off in the hospital bed. After walking past Winston (who barked fiercely at me), I dragged myself upstairs to my room. I just wanted to sleep until we had to show up in court the next morning.

As I stood in the doorway of my room, a chill ran through me. *Who lived here?* The sparseness of the room suggested a kind of barrenness in its occupant; the stuffed animals, the bed covering with the little tassels, and the old toys seemed to belong to someone very young.

That night, I couldn't find the strength to bathe, even though I hadn't done so in almost two weeks. In the same clothes I had worn the night I was taken to the hospital, I climbed into bed and wept.

The following morning, my mother woke me—late, as usual. I looked at the clock; we had only an hour to get to the courthouse. I needed to wash my hair, I told her, as if expecting she would do it for me.

She had bought me a new suit at Jordell's. Though Millie had quit her job there, the owner had always liked her and invited her to continue to use her employee discount. Apparently, the woman was aware of how much Millie spent on clothes.

Before my hospitalization, I'd fallen in love with the outfit—the soft woolen tweed, the matching vest and blazer—but it was too expensive, and Millie reminded me I wouldn't have anywhere to wear it. I had begged her, though, and perhaps owing to her own inability to resist new clothes, she gave in.

When I pulled it from my closet, I remembered how the skirt had fit me snugly; now, I had to pin it to keep it from falling. When I was finally dressed, I felt strange. I felt odd.

In the car on the way to the courthouse, though we were silent, I knew Millie could sense my nervousness. When we reached the courtroom, I was struck by the many faces—all staring at me. Before I could react, Millie turned and walked the other way, disappearing into the lobby. I sat down in the back row until a court guard approached and asked if I was "with them," meaning my father and his lawyer. I nodded, and the guard gently took my arm and walked me past those intense courtroom faces. It must have been my exhaustion that kept me calm.

"We're waiting for you, Tina," said the judge. A tall, slender woman in her mid-forties with coarse dark hair, she looked responsible, able.

"I'd like to speak with you in my chambers," she said. She led me into an office area behind the courtroom, and another woman followed and closed the door behind us.

Inside, the judge pulled up a chair and told me to sit down. "You realize you committed a crime," she said sternly. I was confounded, to say the least.

"It's against the law in the state of Illinois to attempt suicide."

I suddenly realized I was going to jail.

Taking handfuls of my mother's pills had put me in the ranks of thieves and convicts. I was humiliated and embarrassed; it had never occurred to me that I had actually committed a crime. I tried, desperately, to summon the energy to think clearly, but my mind was flooded with images of a different kind of prison.

The judge seemed exasperated. I noticed her fingers, long and thin like my mother's, and I thought she might have a daughter my age—probably in school at that moment, safe and looked after. It was Friday, and I imagined this woman going home after a long day in court to cook dinner for her husband and daughter, thankful she was finished with the likes of me for another day.

"Your father feels it is in your best interest not to live with your mother any longer. He's filed for custody and would like you to live with him." She paused, searchingly.

"How do you feel about that, Tina?" I could only move my head enough to attempt a nod.

So, perhaps I wasn't going to jail after all. My mind was racing.

"I'd rather stay with my mother," I said, but the words came out in a low, uncertain whisper. I suspected the judge might sympathize with this decision.

"I can't allow that," she stated flatly.

Shocked, I found myself wanting to ask about her daughter—if, in fact, she had one.

"If you don't want to live with your father, and you can't live with your mother, what are your alternatives?

I hesitated, struggling to think. Perhaps I could find an apartment for myself? Or, maybe I could live with one of the families Kathryn cared for—my mother could visit often, take me shopping . . . have lunch.

"If you don't decide to have some input on where you live, I will need to send you to a foster home."

I hadn't a clue what she meant by "foster home." When the judge detected this, she explained it was a safe place where I would be looked after properly and provided with food and shelter.

I turned my head to the woman silently typing in a nearby corner; praying for her to say something; to suggest something that could save me.

"She's typing what we say," the judge said, reading my thoughts again; she seemed, quite suddenly, to soften her words.

"Why?" I asked her.

"Everything we discuss will be necessary for the lawyers to go over for their clients—your mother and father."

I was appalled.

"My father is going to know that I don't want to live with him?"

"Do you have any other family members with whom you feel safe?"

I grasped, immediately, that she was granting me another option. "I want to live with my uncle," I said.

"Do you know your uncle well?"

"Yes," I said as I watched the woman type.

"Have you stayed with him before?"

"Yes."

"Look at me when you talk, Tina."

"Yes, this last summer I stayed with my aunt and uncle for two weeks."

"Did you like it there?"

"It was fun," I answered, remembering how I seemed to fit in among their six rambunctious children.

Before dismissing me, the judge asked for the names of my aunt and uncle and the town in which they lived. She seemed pleased that they were close to the northwest suburbs of Chicago, in the same county as the court—a reasonable distance for Alan, as well as a court-appointed lawyer, to visit me.

I was led back into the courtroom and instructed to "stay put." For a moment, I looked around for my mother. She was seated alone at the back of the room, holding her purse tightly on her lap. I hadn't seen my father that day until the judge called him to the stand. His lawyer, a well-dressed man in a dark suit, about the same height and age, stood next to him like a bodyguard. I watched as they spoke discreetly with the judge, occasionally glancing back at Millie, who looked as if she were awaiting a jail sentence. I watched as Alan left the room, apparently to make a telephone call; he soon returned, smiling and chatting pleasantly with the judge.

At my request, temporary custody was granted to my aunt and uncle. This would give the judge more time to review my case, which was, without question, an odd one. On the one hand, Wes was fighting for Millie to retain custody, and Alan hadn't filed for custody when Susan went to live with him. On the other hand, there was my suicide attempt and the obvious signs that something was slightly "off" with my mother.

Later that day, after riding home with Millie, I packed my things into my closet and asked her to save them for me. As I packed, Millie stood over me, occasionally turning to pace, then coming back to watch me sort my things. I felt an aching sense of betrayal amid relief. It was as if my mother and I were breaking up after a long, doomed affair.

She drove me to my junior high school. I walked through the empty hallways to the principal's office, passing classrooms, relieved I was never coming back.

The principal met me at the office and walked me to my locker.

"Is there anyone you want to say goodbye to?" she asked.

I looked straight at her. I suppose it didn't take her long to figure out my answer.

Alan's brother Larry, his wife Brenda, and their six kids lived in a modest two-story home about thirty miles north of Hinsdale. They were practicing Jews and excellent, loving parents who maintained an open-door policy for family.

While awaiting the news on the next court date and the final decision on custody, I went to live with them and enrolled in the local junior high school. Although I was hardly in shape for the transition to a new school and a new environment, Larry, Brenda, and the kids did everything they could to make me feel at home.

Millie had occasionally been around Larry during visits to Alan's mother's house, but she hadn't seen him in years; he knew little about my recent history. Though brothers, Larry and Alan were as different as night and day. Larry, about six-foot-two and two hundred pounds, could be guff and rowdy at times, but his warm poise softened his intimidating presence. A robust man, comfortable in his own skin, Larry was full of compassion and more generous than anyone I'd ever encountered. His kids—my cousins—were a wild bunch, but they all seemed to thrive in the unruly atmosphere of their house.

Upon my unexpected appearance, Uncle Larry announced to everyone, "Tina is going to live with us for a while." My cousin Sabrina, a year older than me, simply said, "Cool."

Within a week, Brenda took the girls and me to the mall to shop for clothes. "You need better-looking stuff than this," said a fashion-minded cousin, referring to the hooded sweatshirt that had become my uniform. "You need to look cool." My two female cousins were delighted to have a new girl in the family to dress and usher around in front of their friends.

What struck me most when I first arrived was the invisible family system in which everyone appeared to operate. Brothers pummeled each other, toppling over in laughter. Sisters talked over one another while making snacks for themselves in the kitchen. Mornings were a three-ring circus, and endless struggle to beat the clock. Brenda, an experienced ringleader and apparent magician, managed to get everyone out the door fed, dressed, and equipped with completed homework and brown-bag lunches.

Moving in with my uncle's family was certainly the best thing that could have happened to me at that point, but I was terrified of not fitting in. Life at their house was like nothing I'd ever seen. Daily dramas and trials were addressed—as a family—around the dinner table; the individual needs and idiosyncrasies of my cousins were attended to as part of a larger whole. I desperately wanted to become a member of this merry clan, but I was intimidated by their closeness, unused to the idea of being in such a seemingly cohesive unit.

Most days, I felt as if I were sitting on the sidelines at an ice rink with a broken skate. I just didn't have the means or the energy to join in the fun.

By Thanksgiving, nearly a month had passed since I'd spoken with my mother, and I asked to visit her, believing that seeing her might quell the building anxiety I felt. I thought if I could reacquaint myself with what was familiar to me, I'd adjust better to my new environment.

Even more importantly, I was deeply worried about Millie. I began to have a growing fear that, if we went much longer without contact, she might simply disappear.

So, I went home for Thanksgiving—against the mandate of the court, which was that I should remain under the constant supervision of my aunt and uncle. No one could blame them for agreeing to my request to see her. After all, she was my mother, it was a holiday, and it had been nearly a month since I'd last seen her.

I remember little about that Thanksgiving visit with Millie; it was nothing out of the ordinary. She spent most of the weekend on the sofa, petting the dog and staring off at the TV while I lay in bed, feeling as if the walls were caving in on me. I'd lost the strong sense of purpose I'd had for years with Millie and that had been the basis of my entire identity.

Clearly I was unable to live with her in that house any longer. The question that plagued me, however, was whether I could live without her.

The Sunday night following Thanksgiving, I returned to my aunt and uncle's, but the next morning, instead of going to school, I wandered off. When the bus pulled up, I had the acute sense that I was too vulnerable to step onto it, that somehow I needed to protect myself, so I instinctively walked away. I have little recollection of where I thought I was going, but when I did the same thing the next day, my aunt and uncle notified the hospital.

"You were walking around, completely out of it," Aunt Brenda told me when I asked about the incident years later. She said my skin had become eerily ashen and that it seemed as if I were in a walking coma. Uncle Larry later described the episode as if I were a soldier back home from war, struggling to return to civilian life.

Aunt Brenda and Uncle Larry had provided a safe, caring environment for me, but I couldn't relax into it. Something in me remained vigilant and kept fighting even after it was no longer necessary.

My mother had said to me that she would be the first to die. Following my failed attempt at suicide, I sensed that somehow, she would follow through on her vow. Seeing her that Thanksgiving weekend, it appeared she'd already begun to do so.

For the first time, Uncle Larry began to understand what I'd endured with Millie. When he left me at the hospital after my second day of wandering off, he wept for a long time.

"I felt helpless," he said. "I felt like I'd come to the end of the road. I didn't know what more I could do."

I'd always dreamt of being in an environment like the one Larry and Brenda offered me but, once I was in it, I had no idea what was expected of me. Removed from Millie, the survival mechanisms I'd spent so long honing just didn't apply. I was left with a profound emptiness and no idea of how to navigate this new world.

8th grade, 1979, 3 weeks before I entered Old Orchard Hospital.

Chapter Fourteen

The Promise of Being Whole Again

On November 30, 1979, five days after my Thanksgiving visit with my mother, I was admitted to Old Orchard Hospital, a 133-bed psychiatric hospital in Skokie, Illinois.

My medical records from the time state, "In October, the patient was rushed to the Hinsdale Hospital when it was found that she had overdosed on twenty-six Fiorinal tablets, which she found in the medicine cabinet and which her mother used for tension headaches. . . . When she was admitted, she was in a catatonic, withdrawn state, reliving the experience with drugs, could not relate to those around her, was becoming less able to be cared for in the home."

During the intake interview at Old Orchard, I was unable to provide the attending social worker with any information. I was incapable of putting together coherent thoughts or recalling anything about my life; I felt as if I were suffering from amnesia. My speech was fragmented, and anything I did manage to say seemed to contribute to the social worker's assessment that I was suffering from a "psychotic condition."

Aunt Brenda and Uncle Larry were with me, but they knew little about my past, so the social worker felt it best to contact other members of my family—specifically, Millie—to compile a more complete history. All my aunt and uncle could say was that while I was living with them, I wandered around, crying and incoherent, and that my state did not seem to be ameliorated by reassurance.

The first week of my hospitalization, the doctors determined that my behavior was "regressive," noting that I spent a good deal of time in the fetal position, whimpering, fearful, and asking for my mother. I was assigned to the fourth floor, a heavily supervised area reserved for children and adolescents deemed a threat to themselves or others. They put me on escape-and-suicide precaution and gave me a low dose of Mellaril, a low-potency antipsychotic drug.

I wanted nothing more than to be left alone in my bed. But because I was on suicide watch, a staff member visited every fifteen minutes. The awareness of being constantly watched brought on acute paranoia in me, and I began to feel as if I were locked in a prison—precisely how I imagined my mother usually felt.

Looking back, I feel that my initial experience in therapy was remarkably similar to being deprogrammed from a cult. The goals of my stay at Old Orchard were to recreate a sense of family and to provide me with support in a safe environment. The hospital was to be a place where I could build self-esteem, learn to communicate more effectively, and be away from the source of my emotional stress—my mother.

Still, I missed her terribly. My thirteen years of living with her gave me little preparation for relationships in the outside world. My identity was so enmeshed with Millie's that, in her absence, I had little knowledge of how to behave in "normal" situations and interpret "normal" emotional responses. When someone treated me nicely, when they complimented me, I grew suspicious—it simply couldn't be *that easy.*

Over the years, whenever life with my mother went well, when she lasted long enough to let me in, my world became more habitable. At those times, I could be filled with such joy that nothing else seemed to compare. Except for these hard-earned victories, I had almost no experience of feeling good about myself.

Though the doctors had little of my medical history, it wasn't difficult for them to see that my relationship with Millie was marked by extreme codependence. So they separated me from her, hoping that this separation would help me establish an independent sense of identity. But asking me to break my bond with my mother was like asking me to cut off my right arm.

For the first month of psychotherapy, I wasn't allowed to see my mother at all. I'd have to acquaint myself with a different reality—one not dictated by Millie.

On the first day of art therapy class, I had to draw a self-portrait. I was certainly no artist, and the stick-figure representation I drew was missing body parts. In my own mind, I lacked any distinguishing features.

One night, my mother successfully got a call through to me at the hospital by claiming to be my aunt. As soon as I heard her voice, I began sobbing and begged her to come and get me.

"Mom," I pleaded. "Please. I can't stay here." I assumed she was calling to get me out. But she replied, "I couldn't get near that place." When the staff noticed I was upset, my telephone privileges were suspended.

Later that night, as visiting hours were starting, I peered out from my room. For a week, I'd been carefully observing the routines of the staff, taking note of who worked which shift and whom I might be able to sneak past. The elevator door opened and, as people stepped out, I stepped in. As the door to the elevator closed, I held my breath, hoping no one had seen me. I was on my way down to the ground floor.

When the doors opened, I got off and made my way toward the main entrance. Head down, hands in the pockets of my sweatshirt, I walked casually past the reception desk. The receptionist was gathering her belongings. When she bent over to pick up her purse, I slipped through the exit. I quickened my pace.

I looked back at the building to make sure I wasn't being followed. As I did, I happened to glance up at my floor. The faces of the other residents were looking out at me, straining to get a glimpse. I started to run.

Once I felt I was a safe distance away, I slowed to catch my breath and tried to determine how far I was from home. It was dusk. A car suddenly came up behind me; I jumped to hide in the shadows, between parked cars.

On the move again, I reached a two-lane highway. I noticed a hospital across the way. I figured I could blend in with the commotion in the lobby of the emergency room enough to make a telephone call. As I neared the busy road, a car screeched to a halt in front of me.

The driver noticed me and had a flirtatious smile as he opened the door to his car. He stepped out and began making his way around to the passenger side where I was standing. I tried to veer around him, but he put his arms out, as if we were simply playing a game.

"Hey," he called. "Hey!"

I ran the other way.

"Slow down," he said. "We can have fun."

Luckily, another car pulled up, distracting the guy's attention and making me aware of the oncoming traffic.

Going back in the direction I had come from was not an option. I looked down at my feet. I was wearing only socks. In the chilly evening air, I could see my breath. I darted across the highway, heading for the bright lights of the hospital parking lot, paying no attention to traffic. I heard, vaguely, honks and squeals and shouts coming from several cars.

When I made it to the nearest telephone booth in the entryway of the hospital, I stepped inside and placed a collect call to my mother. Worried she wouldn't answer, I suddenly realized what I had done. Then she picked up the phone.

"Hello?" She sounded annoyed.

"Mom," I said, out of breath. "I escaped. I got out of there." I was expecting her to offer to come get me, so I began looking around to find landmarks. By now, the moon had risen. I still couldn't tell whether I was close to home.

"No, you didn't," she countered.

"Mom, I did," I said. My voice was shrill. I looked around, trying to come up with something to convince her.

"No, you didn't."

Frustrated, I gave in. "Okay," I said. "You're right. I didn't."

I heard a click. She'd hung up on me.

For a moment, I couldn't move. I stood, telephone hanging at my side, biting my lip to keep from crying. I left the hospital and started walking again, hoping I was going in the right direction.

As I walked farther, I began to see street names that seemed familiar. I noticed my new school. I was close to my aunt and uncle's house!

I neared their house and spotted my uncle walking to his car. I hid behind a bush until he pulled out of the driveway. Once he was down the street, I walked up to the house and went inside. Sabrina, one of my cousins, was on the couch in front of the television, and I sat down next to her.

"You have to go back, you know," she said as I took off my socks, which had holes in them from all the running. She told me the hospital had called. Her father had just driven off to look for me.

As Uncle Larry returned me to the hospital that night, he made it clear he just wanted me to be safe. I wanted him to see that I was safe—on the couch with my cousin. In that moment, I felt resentful about not being able to spend a Saturday evening in front of the TV. But I knew I had to go back. I liked my uncle too much to put up a fight.

In the car, we were quiet. The radio was playing quietly. I wished we could drive a little longer.

"Sweetheart," he finally said to me as he was leaving. "You're going to be okay."

Back at the hospital, a nurse performed a body search on me, and I was given a cup to urinate in. I was restricted to wearing pajamas—without any shoes—and escorted to my room. I sank into bed and quickly fell into a deep sleep for the first time in weeks.

In the morning, the doctor ordered an electroencephalogram (EEG), a test that would monitor my brain waves. I tried to imagine what they would learn from the test. Though they told me it was a "noninvasive" procedure, I worried that they'd see something in my brain that I couldn't hide, something that would make them lock me up for good.

I still hadn't spoken to anyone about life with Millie. I had no idea where to begin. I lacked the words and perspective to describe what it was like living on Vine Street. Looking back, it amazes me that I was scanned by machines, fed medication, restricted to a hospital room—all while my mother's madness deepened and spread like a cancer.

After several attempts, my social worker—who was still trying to gather my medical records—was finally able to get Millie in for an appointment. My mother arrived one day, her old clothes practically hanging off her, Kathryn in tow. I hadn't seen my mother in nearly a month. She'd lost a great deal of weight, and I worried what the staff might think. She appeared terribly troubled, wringing her hands and surveying the room with great obvious anxiety. Kathryn stood by her, quietly, as Millie informed me that she was dying. I looked to my grandmother for some kind of confirmation of what I was hearing but found nothing in her face.

Millie did, at last, provide a more formal history for the staff. The information on record seems to me a testament to how troubled she must have felt during that time. Why the interviewing doctor didn't immediately recognize the seriousness of Millie's own condition after getting a clearer picture of our family, I have no idea. Of course, they knew something was wrong; the pieces were beginning to come together. My erratic behavior, my suicide attempt, Millie's disheveled and paranoid state—clearly, there was evidence of a woman's inability to care for her child.

Millie Smiley, age 38, describes herself as having many illnesses and financial hardships; had heavy physical jobs in which she would feel much fatigue, and is presently under weight [sic] having past illnesses of hypoglycemia, pulmonary thrombus, and varicose veins. She is presently working as a stock woman in a dress store in Hinsdale and states she likes this job because she is surrounded by beautiful clothes. [Millie actually hadn't worked there in years.]

Early in the interview, however, the social worker noted that the information Millie provided was "contradicted" and that "it was very difficult to assess adequately the validity" of her statements and "bring any kind of continuity of thought to the interview." The notes go on to say that "her voice was monotoned [sic] until the very end of the interview" and that it was "quite evident that she was experiencing dryness in the mouth with possible use of medication. However, that is presumption; it can only be noted in the observation of physical appearance." Apparently, Millie added that she had "not been well in years."

Millie also advanced her own theory of why I'd had to be hospitalized. "Brenda was giving her penicillin," she told the social worker. Like much of what she said in the meeting, this statement had no basis in fact.

At different points in the interview, Millie described herself as relatively healthy and me as the one who had been suffering. "Mother states that she doesn't get depressed," Millie went on to say that I didn't "handle sadness or depression well and took to the use of drugs" and that I handled my anxiety by "slamming doors, cracking points off pencils, becoming angry and mean, crude, and calling mother names; the use of vulgarity."

Throughout the interview, a sort of assessment of our family system, Millie mentioned that Alan was often abusive with her, that I was closest to Millie, that Susan—or Susie, as she referred to her—

was "Daddy's little girl," and that Susan and I fought constantly. It's clear that Millie attempted to dissociate herself from what the social worker described as "indications" that we were an "extremely dysfunctional family."

In refusing any responsibility for my situation, Millie clearly had little insight into her own condition and was terrified of being hospitalized herself.

After strapping foam-rubber bats to my arms, a muscular male therapist stood in front of me in the gym, egging me on.

"Come on," he said, taunting me, extending his neck like a chicken pecking at feed. "Hit me."

It was a strange moment. Though I couldn't possibly harm this man, I was terrified of expressing my anger.

What if it consumed me? What if I lost control? Awkwardly, I began to strike him with the foam rubber bats. Perhaps this wasn't the most orthodox of therapies, but expressing anger was part of my therapy, necessary for the separation I had to undergo. It was the first time I was able to safely unleash the rage in me. After a while, when I saw I wasn't going to be punished, that the therapist wasn't going to strike me back, I became less self-conscious, letting him have it and yelling as he encouraged me to do. The anger came from so deep within me that I suddenly grew weak and began to cry.

"Good job," the therapist said, much to my surprise, giving me a quick pat on the back and directing me to the fourth floor.

By Christmas, my depression had subsided some, and I was able to stop medication. The staff had been helping me to vocalize my needs and talk about my feelings, to step out of the shadow I'd been hiding in for years. It seemed almost magical, digging past my self-hatred to underlying causes I could examine with my therapist.

My first battle, the separation from Millie, became less intense because I held on to the hope that I could return to her. When I was actually allowed to express my anger with her, I marveled at my words. Moreover, I had a sympathetic ear, someone who agreed that I'd been treated inappropriately. I began to feel as if I'd been carrying around a sack of stones and was now, stone by stone, lightening my load.

Because of my endurance, I suppose, and the tenacity I exhibited in dealing with my emotions, the staff felt I had made progress and moved me to the third floor, which accommodated "short-timers" and imposed fewer restrictions. During one therapy session, my psychiatrist, with whom I'd been in constant stand-offs (he waited for me to talk, and I wondered what to talk about), asked, "Did your mother ever do anything to make you mad?" I thought about this and knew what he was trying to get at, but felt manipulated.

"No," I said smugly.

He persisted, trying to find a point of weakness in me.

"Does your mother love Winston more than she loves you?"

That question was less easy to ignore. I felt my cheeks burn red and my stomach start to tense.

"No," I managed to reply.

"Well, doesn't she?" he said, looking at me with raised eyebrows.

For a long while, I said nothing. *So, yeah, what if she does,* I thought. *What if my mother loves her stupid dog more than she loves me?* I was getting tired of this.

"Aren't you mad at what she did to you?"

I jumped out of my chair, got right up in his face, and yelled, "You can't tell me how to feel!"

Fine. He won. He'd made me angry.

"Are you sure you're not mad at your mother?"

"No!" I screamed. "I'm not!"

"Well, you sure aren't acting like you're not."

I hit the wall with my fist, gritting my teeth as I looked at him. "No, no, no, I'm not!" I shuddered at the sound of my own voice, hardly recognizing what I was saying or where in me the emotions had come from.

A staff member ran into the room, asking if anyone needed assistance. The psychiatrist told him to leave, and then turned back to me.

"Tell your mother how you feel, Tina."

I looked at him for a long time.

"I hate the way you smoke," I said in a whisper, my eyes tearing. "I hate it. I can't stand it." The psychiatrist nodded at me, and I wanted to punch him.

"I hate the way you clear your throat and the way you pet that stupid dog of yours." I felt stupid, but something in me wanted to continue. "I hate that house and every day there. I can't stand it anymore."

By the time I finished, my voice cracked, and I broke down in tears. "Why doesn't she love me?" I asked. The crying turned into a deep sobbing that didn't want to end. I looked up at the psychiatrist.

"Why can't she just love me?"

In a journal that I kept during the time, I wrote,

> *Why don't I realize what my mother did to me? Is it because I protected her for 13 years and she didn't protect me so I built up a great wall saying I was the mom of the home. What is it? It's going to take so long to straighten out... Why couldn't Grams have taught her how to clean, how to cook, how to take care of herself.*

I began talking with some of the other "short-term" residents who were in the hospital for similar reasons: to learn how to cope with stress, build self-esteem and a sense of belonging, improve family relationships and develop "normal" social interactions. These were tall orders for us. But in recognizing the same reactions in others my age, I felt a camaraderie I had never experienced among "normal" children in the classroom or in my isolation with Millie.

I was fine-tuning my emotions and, in many ways, the other patients became my models. I envied their tears, which I no longer saw as a sign of weakness but as a way of fighting for what they had, which was their very selves. I made distinctions between anguish—something I had long experienced in Millie's house—and sadness, the letting go of what I had lived through. I told a staff member that I would deal with things the way they were, not the way I wanted them to be.

By the end of December, I was allowed supervised visits with Millie. The next court date had been postponed until the staff could gather more details about my progress. When she and Kathryn visited on New Year's Eve, Millie begged me to answer just one question: "Who do you want to live with?"

Sitting there in front of me, Millie appeared smaller, as if she had not only lost weight but also managed to shrink somehow. The terrain of her face had changed. Her features protruded oddly, giving her an eerie appearance.

Even though I knew my returning to live with her was unlikely, I simply said, "Of course I want to come home."

Afterward, the supervisor asked why I didn't express my anxiety about the custody case to my mother. I was afraid of hurting her, I explained, and worried that she might hurt herself if I told her I didn't want to live with her. During our visit, Millie had referred to death and dying several times. She'd look off into the distance and become expressionless. "I'll die in my sleep," she said. I tried practicing what they had taught me in therapy. "Don't talk that way," I said to her. Although it was a meek attempt, I was trying to let her know there'd be no going back home with her if she couldn't hold up her end of the bargain, but she didn't—or couldn't—pick up on my cues.

The first court hearing had neither restored parental rights to Millie nor awarded custody to my father. I was appointed a lawyer, who visited with me at the hospital. Periodically, he'd ask me if I "felt better" about my father. I can't say I was ever truthful with my lawyer, but I was tired of being stuck in the middle. I wanted to know that when I left the hospital, I'd have a place to go where I could be near Millie but would no longer be responsible for her care. My psychiatrist knew my options were limited. My stay with my uncle was never meant to be long term; given what everyone had seen of Millie, it was most likely that I would have to live with my father.

Two days after Millie's visit to the hospital, I received a letter from her. I opened it excitedly, half-hoping that it was now safe for me to go home, that she'd taken care of everything and we could go on with our lives.

"When I die," she wrote, "I want you to cremate my body and spread my ashes over the Pacific Ocean."

The letter was still in my hands when my doctor, making his rounds, came in. He asked what had happened. All I could think of was her frail body and that agonized look on her face. She was sending me a message. She needed me to save her.

> *Dear Mom,*
> *I was upset on the phone when I talked with you because I miss you and love you so much. It's hard being away from you. I hope everything is O.K. I'm O.K. You heard the court date was postponed until Dr. K. gives a full report on how well I'm doing. . . . I feel like slapping Dad in the face. The court is making me upset. I wish it would just get over with. [sic] You really have to change for me to come home. You have to start acting like my mother. You have to take care of me. You have to make more stricter [sic] rules. Change for me, okay. Kathy [a staff member] said I would be a swell mother because I would know the mistakes. I really love you. I better be coming home soon.*

During Mill's next visit, when I asked about her last letter, she explained, matter-of-factly, that she had just seen a show about funeral rip-offs on television. She simply didn't want Susan and me to have to pay too much to bury her.

By Valentine's Day 1980, four months after my suicide attempt, signs of hope were beginning to emerge for me. I was angry at being in the middle of parents' hatred for one another, tired of Millie's inability to care for me, fed up with what I saw as my father's mixed messages. I was allowing myself to ask for—and even expect—things and learning to find constructive ways of getting my needs met. I had developed a few friendships with other patients and was finally given permission to go about my day unsupervised. I started developing a faith I had never before possessed.

In the absence of my mother, I had made some strides, and I slowly began to realize the dangers of returning to her. I imagined scenarios in which I could begin a new life with Alan and his family and reunite with my sister. I felt the only chance I had to hold on to my newfound courage was to live in a household resembling those I thought everyone else had during my childhood. I wanted to blend into a family's daily routine without causing any ripples.

Of course, I thought, I would visit Millie on weekends, letting her know I still loved her and helping her find what I had found through therapy.

At the beginning of March 1980, a week shy of my fourteenth birthday, my doctor informed me that the court had granted custody to my father. Despite my earlier feelings of excitement at the prospect of starting a new life with Alan, Nancy, and Susan, I suddenly felt terrified. For all I had learned, for all the progress I had made, I still felt raw and unready.

In one of my last sessions at Old Orchard Hospital, Alan and Nancy—my new official parents—showed up, but I felt as if there was a world between us.

I looked directly at Alan in a way I knew he couldn't reciprocate.

"How do you see me?" I asked nervously.

"Well," he started, as I bit my lip, "I think you're very stubborn and inconsiderate. You don't think about how other people feel." He added that in order for me to come live with him, I'd have to "change my attitude."

I was devastated. In just seconds, all my progress seemed to have fallen to pieces.

"No," I said, fiercely. "I won't come live with you. I'll kill myself before I come live with you."

Frustrated, Alan retorted. "Well, if you do, finish the job. I'm not going to go through this shit again."

When Susan interviewed Alan nearly twenty-five years later, she asked him what his best advice was to her and me.

"Get some real deep-down therapy. Blood and guts. Absolutely blood and guts . . . Get in there and scream, yell, holler, kick the walls, kick the people . . . and get to the primal issues at hand of why your dad left and you felt abandoned and why your mother dealt with you the way she dealt with you.

"The crime, if there is one, is the fact that two children were not nurtured in a loving, wholesome, intellectual environment. Just a constant chaos of emotion . . . lack of support . . . no love."

The prognosis when I left Old Orchard was, "Guarded. This family situation is so unpredictable, inconsistent, and unreliable that prognosis is unclear. Good discharge planning will be important."

On May 16, 1980, I was discharged.

Chapter Fifteen

Earning My Keep

I was fourteen when I moved into Alan and Nancy's house in a well-to-do suburb of Chicago about twenty miles from Hinsdale. Shortly thereafter, I began attending high school in Oak Park, a neighboring town, famous as the home of Frank Lloyd Wright and the birthplace of Ernest Hemingway.

While I tried to focus on my new situation, I still worried constantly about my mother. I was terrified that without me, she wouldn't survive, that she'd die alone on Vine Street.

Though Millie had been advised by my social worker to return to Old Orchard Hospital for counseling, she never did. While I was making progress, she was languishing; I felt very guilty about this. I knew that, as her ally, I understood her better than anyone else. I didn't want to leave her behind.

"What would have happened if I did die when I wanted to?" I wrote in my journal around that time. "What would my mother have done? Feed on Susie or on the dog? The only people left were the dog and Grams, who she despises from her childhood."

One by one, family members had left—each departure leaving an even greater burden on those who remained behind. First Alan, then Susan, and now me; the family had disintegrated, and only Millie was left.

One afternoon, several weeks after I began staying with Alan's family, Millie's cousin Nancy called; I happened to answer the telephone. My mother had been in a car accident. She'd driven into a telephone pole and was in the intensive care unit (ICU) at Hinsdale Hospital.

"She broke a few ribs," Nancy continued, "and she's going to need some stitches on her face. She's asking for you."

As the nightmarish words started to sink in, my heart began to race; I looked around the room, trying to think of how I could get to her.

That evening, when my father got home from work, I was told that I was no longer allowed to answer the telephone, nor should I ask about Millie or try to visit her. If I disobeyed, I'd be sent back to Old Orchard—or a permanent detention center. I think Alan and Nancy believed that if I stopped thinking about my mother and got on with my life, all my problems would just go away.

For weeks after the accident, I was unable to concentrate on anything. I had nightly terrors about my mother—alone in the hospital, asking for me, hurt by my failure to respond to her. The guilt I felt was almost unbearable. But what if I did escape and went to her? I'd be risking any chance for a normal life with Alan and Nancy. Despite all the work I'd done in therapy, and even though I recognized Millie was unable to take care of me—and had actually harmed my sister and me—nothing could break my loyalty to her.

Millie was always a bad driver, and her thrill-seeking led to more than a few small mishaps over the years. One time, she took me to buy a ten-speed bike with handlebar brakes. When we got it home, she reminded me that she hadn't ridden a bike in a long time. I had a hard time picturing her on a bike, so I told her to try it. She looked a little like a young Katharine Hepburn as she rode down the driveway toward the garage, her legs out in front of her.

"Where the hell are the brakes?" she yelled suddenly, but it was already too late. She crashed into the back wall of the garage and came away limping, swearing she'd never get on a bike again. And she didn't. But she was a thrill seeker, racing the local college boys on the highway in our Volkswagen Beetle. She did it for laughs more than anything else. Luckily, no one ever got hurt.

But when I was told that she was in the ICU, I knew something had gone terribly wrong. This wasn't one of her minor accidents or a racing game gone awry. I suspected her condition had begun to deteriorate seriously.

While I was living with her, Millie was always in jeopardy, but then I was near her, attempting to care for her and trying to control the situation. Now, out of touch and far away, I just felt helpless. Slowly, however, I began to realize that, for all her complaints about me, she wasn't getting any better in my absence. From a distance and with my new perspective, I started to see that I *wasn't* causing my mother's grief; it was something deep within her.

As in the past, Susan's solution was to stay away as often as possible, busying herself with after-school activities, friends, schoolwork, and part-time jobs. My approach to a difficult home environment hadn't changed much, either. I tried not to ask for much or provoke anyone; though the emotional cost of holding it all in was enormous, I did my best to become a ghost in the house.

One day, out of frustration, perhaps just overwhelmed by taking in two troubled children, Alan's wife Nancy told me that I would grow up, get divorced, and beat my children if I didn't "get my act together." I wonder, now, if she was actually worried about herself and simply projecting this fear onto me. I wrote a note in a journal to reassure myself:

> *I know I'm a survivor. My stepmother said to me that I will grow up and beat my children and get a divorce. That won't happen because I'll make a great mother or I won't get married.*

In another entry, I described my frustration with my stepmother:

> *My stepmother started talking to me. Then yelling. The words finally came out. "Tina, you're such a failure." It struck me like a bullet in my head. I'd never recover. I sat in my bathroom saying to myself, "You're not a failure. You're a good person. Don't listen." I said that to myself for days. I said to myself, "You won't give up. You'll put up a fight." I tried so hard to get myself to think that I was good, but I couldn't get those words out of my mind. . . . I did try. . . . If I were to get one wish or get one present in my life it would be a kiss, hug, and I love you. I never did get any, and I still don't. I have to make the move. I have to say "I love you" so someone will say "I love you" back to me. I really never had a mother like that. Maybe they're extinct. I know my stepmother has something. She does with her children all the time. Every time I see her hug and kiss them, I always say, will I be next. But I never do get any. It's as if I'm invisible. I've tried my hardest to do my best. All I ever wanted was an "I love you."*

What stayed with me, what sustained me most days, was the vision I'd experienced in the hospital after my suicide attempt. Regardless of whether I had imagined it, as long as I believed in it, I had a reason to go on.

Susan and I knew that in order for us to live with Alan and Nancy's family, we had to expect little for ourselves; having grown up with Millie, we'd had plenty of practice doing this. Though we rarely asked for anything, our half-siblings sensed our need. It was as if we had it written all over us; we were hungry for acceptance, encouragement, and unconditional love. Naturally, the other children must have felt threatened and suspicious—perhaps even displaced—when we came to live in their house.

Although my therapist emphasized the importance of including the other children in family therapy, I always went alone. The message was clear: My issues were solely my own.

After one session that Alan had attended with me, I tried to continue a conversation we'd started at the therapist's office. We were in the basement, where he was having a hot tub built, and we were sitting on the floor, amid all the construction. He was about to go out for more supplies, and I was telling him that I thought Nancy was alienating me from the family. I suggested that she wasn't aware she was doing it; I was trying to be fair and wanted him to hear me out. It was the first time we were actually able to talk like this, and I feared that he'd jump up and leave at any moment. But he stayed and listened to me.

It was impromptu; I had a lot I wanted to say, but instead I just talked about Nancy. I asked if he thought Nancy disliked me or if it was all in my head.

"I'm not sure what to do about it," I told him. "I'm trying my best."

Before I could finish, Nancy came into the basement, and Alan immediately revealed to her what I'd been saying. She glared at me, and then sent me to my room.

One of the few things that kept me going during that time was living in the same house as my sister, but my relationship with Susan never seemed to improve. Despite the hopes I had for our reunion, especially away from Millie, she remained shut down, trying to separate from me and from our past. We were quiet around each other, as if we were strangers. Perhaps Alan was right in what he told Susan years later: We each had to save ourselves. Susan seemed to be doing everything she could to save herself.

Alan told Susan that it was, essentially, our responsibility to get to the core of things. He believed—strongly—that he'd come to our rescue, that he was doing us a favor by bringing us to live with him. What we needed was provided. But it always came at a price.

So we began working to earn our keep. Every day after school, I came home and cleaned the house, set the dinner table, and washed the dishes. When I moved in, he told me, in no uncertain terms, that I would not get any money for clothes or lunch because he had already paid enough to "get my head straight." If I needed something, I was told, "Get a job."

The first summer, I got a job washing windows for the neighbor next door. Then, I began cleaning another neighbor's house. Susan had already been working after school behind the counter at a candy shop, then she started waiting tables at a local diner on weekends.

When I turned sixteen, I started working at a Baskin-Robbins several nights a week after school. Susan had begun applying to colleges, and I was terrified at the prospect of her leaving, so I enrolled in an after-school nurse assistant training program and took a job at a nursing home. I wasn't allowed to have a driver's license, so occasionally I got rides from an instructor who found out I'd been riding my bike to work all winter. The job enabled me to be away from home more often and to get Alan off my back about money. During my junior and senior years of high school, I was able to buy my own clothes, have some extra spending money, and rely less on Alan and Nancy.

Because of the barriers of resentment built between "Millie's daughters" and the rest of the family, I made several attempts to help all of us "bond." I knew of a nearby amusement park, so I told my stepmother I thought it might be good for all of us to go. Sometimes Nancy took us all to the opera, but I thought this would be a good way to connect in a less confining place. Taking a day trip together struck me as something that could take us out of the rigid identities and roles we each maintained. To my surprise, Nancy agreed that it was a good idea and said she'd think about it.

Later in the summer, Alan brought home a truckload of bushes he wanted to plant along the border of the property; he was always looking for ways to enhance our privacy. I was given the job of digging trenches around the perimeter of the yard—about one acre. It took me several weeks (though other people pitched in on occasion), working every day after school when I wasn't at my job. Susan helped when she could, but she was still writing college essays and working most nights waiting tables.

While I was digging those trenches, I began to calculate the time it would take me to reimburse Alan for paying my hospital bills and providing a home until I was old enough to be on my own. My digging began to take on a meditative quality. I recalled my vision and realized that it was my only cause for hope. Yes, Aunt Brenda and Uncle Larry had been there for me, and Millie had vowed to help me escape, but not much had really changed. As far as I could see, I'd moved from one type of abusive situation to another.

One day, while I was knee-deep in soil, Nancy left with the kids. At nightfall, when I went inside to wash up, they were just coming in the door. One of them mentioned where they had been that day: Great America, an amusement park I had suggested we visit as a family.

Alan kept Susan and me at a distance by reminding us that Millie was "crazy" and a "lunatic," making a face at the mere mention of her name. He let us know whenever we were "acting like Millie"—something to be avoided at all costs. I had inherited my hearty laugh from my mother and, though I laughed infrequently in those days, I recall a time when I laughed aloud during dinner one night.

"Stop it!" Alan shouted at me, the table quickly growing silent. "You sound just like your mother."

What must my stepsiblings have thought of this woman, my mother? They became suspicious of Susan and me, born to the woman forever known in Alan and Nancy's house as crazy and ill-mannered.

What I began to understand was that, at some point, Alan stopped seeing me at all—if he'd actually ever really seen me, ever really known me. He was seeking absolution for his past with Millie, and Susan and I were in the way. The sense I had living in his house was that Susan and I were stains on the picture he was trying to create with his new family.

Because Alan worked long hours, Nancy struggled to raise the four of us kids, and she always seemed stressed about something, overwhelmed. Nancy prided herself on being the perfect mother; in many ways she was—to her own children. But with Susan and me around, it was hard to maintain that image. After all, raising two children who are not your own and who come with enough baggage to fill the house is no small order.

When she entered her senior year of high school, Susan began expressing interest in moving to New York City to pursue an acting career. At seventeen, Susan was tall, graceful, and willowy. She had

Millie's features—blue eyes, high cheekbones, and fair complexion. Susan had always been modest, which seemed to work against her at times; some people perceived her as aloof. She certainly could use her natural reserve to distance herself from others, which only served to make Nancy more frustrated with her.

Susan came home from crying one day, worried that something was wrong with her. Nearly all her girlfriends had gotten their first periods; even I had started getting my period by that point, though Susan and I never really confided in each other on such matters. I was ten when I frantically informed my mother that I was "hemorrhaging." I remember how she drove me straight to Kathryn's, perhaps feeling unprepared to deal with a menstruating child, announcing to her mother that I had "the curse," laughing and saying I would now become "one of those terrible bitches, like the rest of the family."

I was in the kitchen washing dishes when I overheard Susan talking to Nancy and wished that Susan had come to me instead. She and Nancy went into the other room, and I could hear Nancy tell her she was being outrageous. Nancy insisted she stop being petty. Eventually, she convinced Alan that Susan was troublesome, perhaps suicidal.

Alan approached Susan and told her that something needed to be done. Susan was wreaking havoc in his home, causing Nancy to be upset all the time. So Susan suggested she move in with one of her friends. But when Nancy heard this, she insisted Susan belonged in Old Orchard—the psychiatric hospital where I'd spent several months.

At the time, Susan was doing well in her classes. She also was in the school musical, ran on the track team, and had many friends. Regardless, Nancy made an appointment for Susan at the hospital. There, they met with the same psychiatrist I had been assigned to; Nancy told him that Susan was depressed and suicidal with psychotic tendencies. While I don't believe Susan was exhibiting signs of depression that warranted hospitalization—she was active, social, and healthy—she had never been to see a therapist or counselor, and I thought it would be a good idea for her to see one. But Nancy insisted that Susan be hospitalized, so she was, involuntarily. She ended up staying four months.

By the time Susan returned from the hospital, she had missed a good part of the fall term. She was out of shape for track and had completely shut down emotionally and socially. She barely said a word to anyone.

Around that time, I stopped therapy but was terrified that Alan and Nancy would try to send me to the inpatient ward also. So I stayed away from Susan and stayed after school more. I thought of myself as a source of constant agitation in the house; staying away seemed to keep everyone happier. If I could come home after dinner, having done my homework at school, and slink into bed without anyone seeing me, then it was a good day—a day without arguments.

One time, Nancy found me crying in my room. I'd been having a bout of loneliness, missing Millie, and was confused about where I belonged. I'd been trying hard to stay out of everyone's way, yet I always seemed to instigate a lot of anger.

"Shape up, Tina," she told me. Alan often said the same thing to me, using military jargon as if they expected me, still a young girl, to simply harden myself against sadness and grief.

Ironically, I did end up doing just that: I joined the military. It was a way for me to run away. But I also felt it was something I'd be good at, something I could call my own. I signed up for basic training and was sent to Fort Dix, New Jersey, for the summer. For once, I gained Alan's approval, and that meant a great deal to me. He would tell me how "cool" he thought it was for a woman to be a soldier.

If this is what it would take to make Alan happy, to make him see me, so be it.

Alan opposed Susan's attending college for liberal arts and fought bitterly with her about it. He simply saw no point in it, and he didn't want her "wasting his money" on something that wasn't, in his view, a serious pursuit. He wanted her to learn a "skill" or a "trade," something practical, but she argued that she didn't want to be a "carpenter or a plumber." This argument went on for weeks.

Nancy stepped in and told Susan her grades weren't good enough for college and that Alan was right. The three of them fought about the same issues repeatedly, day after day. Nancy would yell at Susan for something she had said (or for being unpleasant or unappreciative). Susan and Nancy would bicker; Alan would become disgusted and walk away. Meanwhile, the other children and I would try to stay out of the way, hoping Susan would just go away soon and that the arguing would end.

Susan, however, was determined. She tried applying for loans, but Alan's income was too high; the college wouldn't accept "none of your business" as an answer to how much money our father earned. Alan told her he had spent her education money at Old Orchard Hospital.

Susan did end up going to the University of Illinois—the school where Alan and Millie met—and worked two jobs to cover the cost of her tuition. Although I worried terribly that she was working herself to the bone, I was proud of her. She wasn't going to let anyone break her spirit. It was the legacy we'd been given.

Millie, the summer after I moved in with my father. 1980.

Chapter Sixteen

The Last Days on Vine Street

In the summer of 1983, Millie made a serious attempt to kill herself. At home by herself one night, she slashed her throat and wrists and ingested large amounts of Librium, diuretics, and rubbing alcohol. At some point, she called the police, and they brought her to Hinsdale Hospital, where I'd been taken after my suicide attempt. A few days later, Kathryn went back to the house and dutifully cleaned the blood off the walls and floors. She would never be able to rid her mind of the gruesome scene she found there.

The medical report from Hinsdale stated that Kathryn provided the doctor with a brief history that was "vague and quite unprecise" but suggested that Kathryn no longer denied her daughter's condition. It continued, "Alert, white female with unfashionably long hair who appears thin and somewhat pale. The patient gave suspiciously positive forward-looking answers about everything and then slipped with saying things like there are times when she wanted to die with her dog."

A new psychiatrist at the hospital, Dr. Klempner, gave Millie a nebulous initial diagnosis: "affective disorder." However, he also wrote in his medical notes, "Information from her is vague and circumstantial—making one think of residual schizophrenia." He said the first priority was to treat her wounds from the suicide attempt, many of which were quite serious: several cut tendons and lacerated flexor surfaces on both wrists, an exposed left carotid sheath in her neck. In other words, she had almost cut through one of her main arteries. His second priority was the establishment of a diagnosis.

"Affect," he wrote, "is somewhat silly—inappropriate given the gravity of her attempt." In her chart, he began writing the word "schizo," then scribbled it out and wrote, instead, "affective disorder."

However, soon Millie was back in the hands of Dr. Swanson, her long-time psychiatrist; his diagnostic impression was "schizoaffective disorder with depressed mood." He noted that Millie told him, "The average person would not be here with what I've done. No, I won't tell you what I've done. It's none of your beeswax." In the next line, he went on to say, "Patient was under my care in 1968."

Clearly, Dr. Swanson was not putting all the pieces together. Each time he saw Millie over fifteen years, he seemed to treat her episodes as isolated incidents. When Dr. Klempner saw Millie, he did mention her previous visits with Dr. Swanson but noted that it was "unclear how many previous visits she has had."

Four days after first seeing Millie, Dr. Klempner wrote, in a separate record, "Given patient's history of mood swings with irritability, verbal hyperactivity, poor judgment alternating with periods of hypersomnia, fatigue, weight loss [Millie weighed only one hundred pounds at the time of admission; at five-foot-eight, she appeared skeletal], etc., it is possible that this lady has some variant of bipolar disorder." He mentioned her resistance to treatment, suspected her need for long-term hospitalization, and had her transferred to Madden Zone Center.

Madden, unlike Hinsdale, was a state-funded mental hospital; Millie was transferred there because her public aid wouldn't cover a stay at Hinsdale Hospital, and she had no money. One day, Kathryn and John came to Madden to bring her some clothes. John recalls a nurse greeting them by saying, "She shouldn't be getting a free ride. She lives in Hinsdale and should be paying her bills while she's here." Little did that nurse know that Millie had been stealing and living on cheese, vitamins, and diet pills (to curb her appetite). She had been trying to subsist on $200 a month in public aid. Kathryn had been paying Millie's mortgage; when John learned of this, he exploded in rage.

Doctors at Madden relied largely on Millie's own recollections for her medical history because there was little on file prior to her suicide attempt. Not surprisingly, the information they collected was somewhat dubious. They recorded that she had "two aunts who have mental problems" when there was only one—Aunt Libby—as far as we knew and that her mother was "living but is seriously ill;" Kathryn, at that time, was perfectly healthy and as strong as ever.

Although the records indicate that a lithium trial was in order and that long-term hospitalization was needed, Millie was discharged after only one month at Madden, with little follow-up. "Client is able to sit down now and talk about her feelings and what her plans are for the future," read the last two lines of her Madden medical report, written at discharge. "She is able [to] accept herself as she is and not what she would like to be."

In Susan's film *Out of the Shadow*, Millie talks about her suicide attempt, saying that it took her a while to realize what she'd done. "Things in my brain," she said, "just weren't connecting." After the attempt, she got off all the drugs. "I don't know what came over me. I knew I had to stop taking all those horrendous tranquilizers. I needed to clean out my system." She threw out all the chemicals in the house. All that remained, she said, were "Bactine, Tylenol, rubbing alcohol, peroxide, coffee, vinegar, and ammonia.

"The noise pollution was awful. It was like ten billion years of hell slamming through my head. I think the circuitry missed a connection or something. The police are mad at me to this day—they say they don't want anything to do with that 'bloodbath woman.' I got mad at them for calling me the 'bloodbath woman.' I told them they should do something about their Creepsville problems. Try to clean up Illinois and make it a more livable state."

When Millie was released from Madden, she asked John to pick her up and drive her home. She recalls that very little was said during the ride. Around that time, Kathryn called Millie to tell her she was selling her house to move into something smaller with less upkeep. Millie, beginning to realize the burden she'd been on Kathryn for so many years, promptly told her mother, "Forget it. I'm going to California."

Millie had always talked about going to California, especially when she was in the mood to blame all her problems on the state of Illinois. "People in California are so much nicer," she'd say. "They don't talk about you there just because you're not like them." For Millie, I think California represented a kind of Utopia where people didn't judge others or insist on conformity. In this way, she came to believe that Illinois was responsible for putting her on all the drugs she was taking, that it wanted her to "conform." This, according to Millie, was the reason for the daily hell she lived in.

"They don't know what they're doing," she'd say, though it was never clear who "they" were. "I get pushed around and forced [to use] drugs and told to do this and told to do that. Social Security hounds me. I'm never free." So that was her justification, in part, for wanting to move to another state. In California, she figured, she could stay with some of her father's relatives until she found a place of her own.

Within weeks, Millie put our house on Vine Street on the market and sold it for about $70,000, far below its 1983 market value in Hinsdale.

Millie put almost everything she owned into storage, keeping only the few things she planned to take with her. With the money from the sale of the house, she bought a new Ford Escort station wagon.

Her days on Vine Street were over.

Our home on Vine Street

When I returned to Alan's home after basic training at Fort Dix, living there became unbearable for me. It was clear to me that my presence continued to upset the equilibrium of the house. I felt more out of place, more in the way, than ever.

So I finished high school early and entered Advanced Individual Training (AIT) at Fort Sam Houston in San Antonio, Texas—one of the main army bases for medical-related training. But AIT lasted only a few months and then I landed back at Alan's, facing the same old issues.

I wrote a letter to Susan explaining that I needed to get out. I wanted somewhere else to go but, unlike Susan, I wasn't confident that I could get into college; the application process was terribly daunting to me.

Susan encouraged me to apply to a junior college in Champaign, the same town where she went to school. On the application, I checked off "nursing" as my field of study. It seemed like the most obvious choice for me.

Susan also thought that it was time for me to get away. "Mom tried to kill herself," she told me. It had happened between my junior and senior years of high school, while I was away at Fort Dix.

When I heard this, something in me failed to—or was unable to—respond. I had been trying so hard to remain stoic, to bury my feelings while living with Alan and Nancy, that I suppressed anything I felt about my mother's suicide attempt. I was terrified that if I allowed myself to react, to feel, I would simply break down and would never be able to get back to the place I had worked so hard to reach. Susan tried, with little success, to reassure me that Millie was doing better; she had sold the house, had bought a new car, and was moving to California.

Once, during this period, Millie drove over to Alan and Nancy's to see me, but for the second time, she was turned away.

"Drive safely," Alan said as she walked away. "Get a husband and get a job."

If I showed any hint of missing Millie and Susan, Alan and Nancy took it as a sign of regression. They had been given strict orders by my psychiatrist not to let me have contact with Millie. But I was moving out, and they'd have little recourse if they found out I had contacted her.

On the night I was to leave, I called Millie and discovered she hadn't yet left for California. She was delighted to hear from me and offered to drive me to Champaign (where I was to begin studies at Parkland College) on her way out West. I couldn't understand how things had managed to line up this way for us but, of course, I agreed. I had only a few things with me, planning to move the rest later, once I found an apartment. Alan, Nancy, and the children were out that night, so I took the risk of asking Millie to come and pick me up.

She pulled up in her new car, packed to the roof with boxes, bags, and blankets. I tried to joke with her. "Going camping, Mom?" But then I caught a glimpse of the scars on her neck and was afraid I might pass out. In the passenger seat with my belongings, I had just enough room to sit, my legs crunched in front of me. Millie didn't make any attempt to hide her scars, nor did she say anything about her hospitalization. I didn't bring up the topic, either.

Surprisingly, she was in the best of moods, lighter in many ways than I'd ever seen her. Although racked with anxiety—*Would I ever see her again? Would she be okay driving out there alone? Was she going to be safe in California?*—I was careful not to show it. She seemed genuinely happy, but I knew how fragile such moods could be, and I didn't want to chance bringing her down.

We drove for a long time, chatting, laughing. *When had she become so happy?*

"I'm glad for you, Mom," I told her, sincerely. I turned to face her but still kept an eye on the road, mindful of the drag races during past car trips.

"Oh, I know," she chirped. She told me she had her transcripts with her and would finish college in California.

"I have relatives there, you know," she added, and mentioned that she was looking forward to making new friends.

When we arrived at Susan's, Millie said a quick good-bye to both of us, and then she was off, her red car flashing down the road. I had a sinking feeling in my stomach but tried to explain it away. I just missed her, I reassured myself, and would miss her more when she was halfway across the country. I tried hard not to think about all the bad things that could happen to her.

For the weeks to come, I comforted myself with what she told me in the car. She was going to finish school and "get on and live a normal life."

I hoped she could.

I stayed with Susan for a few nights in Champaign until I was able to find a room in a house not far away. I signed up for two classes and took a job as a phlebotomist at a blood bank, where I worked about thirty hours a week.

I thought often of my mother's many attempts to complete college, and while I could relate to the exhaustion she had felt, I was determined to finish the semester, to prove that I could do well on my own. After all, Susan was doing it, though she was usually too busy even to meet for dinner. On the few occasions when Susan and I did see each other, she made it clear that, though she was happy I was attending college and working, she really didn't want me around. She was working hard, both in school and on herself, and she needed separation and distance from me in order to sort through things.

Clearly, we both needed some space, but Susan had never had this kind of time alone before, and she desperately needed to create a place for herself, away from her past. I'd hoped we could support one another in our new lives. While I felt inadequate, unworthy, and miserable around Alan, I thought my sister and I could truly be ourselves with each other. Only the two of us knew the pain we'd endured. But at the time, talking about our shared pain seemed as if it might keep us mired in it, so we avoided discussing it. Both of us were desperate to prove ourselves, to put Vine Street permanently behind us.

While I was studying at Parkland, I returned to Chicago one weekend a month for army reserve meetings. I would travel on Fridays and arrive at the Greyhound bus station well past midnight, after the commuter train had stopped running for the evening. If I was lucky, I caught a taxi. But on some nights, the only way I could get to my father's house (where I spent the night before weekend drill) was to take the subway to O'Hare Airport and backtrack by taxi, using precious cash. A colonel in my unit who lived nearby drove me, on Saturday mornings, from Alan's to the north side of Chicago. This colonel drove a big Cadillac and smoked cigars; by the time we got to our meeting, I would be sick from the smoke and exhausted from all the traveling. I began asking around to find an alternative. I was told Sergeant Jeff Kotulski, who lived south of Champaign, was willing to drive me to our drills.

Jeff and I began driving to meetings together on those long, cold Friday afternoons in his blue AMC Concord without a heater. He was good-natured and had a phenomenal sense of humor. When I'd get into his car, bundled in scarves and mittens, he'd crack a joke, then smile at me in a way that warmed me more than all those clothes ever could. As if he could sense my nervousness, he assured me it was no problem to pick me up.

I was nineteen at the time and, though a few years older than me, he was just beginning his studies in sports medicine at George Williams College in Downers Grove, Illinois. He talked often of his dream of going to medical school. Very short on cash, I paid my share of gas and tolls by typing various reports for him on a small portable typewriter.

I knew from the start how I felt about him and, though I thought it was written all over my face, I tried to hide my feelings, struggling a great deal with the thought of letting someone into my life. But Jeff demanded a certain integrity from me, and it wasn't my style to play hard-to-get (actually, I don't think I could have even if I'd wanted to). I just worried about the toughness I'd developed over the years, the armor I had built up. With Jeff, I'd eventually have to find a way to shed my protection. Over a period of about three months, as we got to know each other, I grew even fonder of him. My weeks in Champaign began to feel impossibly long as I looked forward to Jeff's monthly arrival and the time we'd spend together.

Whatever Jeff knew about me then, he gave me the sense that nothing about my past could shock him. I joked with him, as I'd done in early years with Millie and he responded by laughing, bantering, and egging me on.

"You're too much," he'd say. I could see that he liked me, but I had to remind myself constantly of that fact; I was doing fine, I wouldn't "screw it up." This was my chance, I thought, to recreate myself. I didn't have to be limited by my past.

After reserve duty one Saturday evening, Jeff asked if I wanted to learn to drive; he even generously volunteered his car.

"Are you sure?" I asked, terrified at the thought.

He nodded. Jeff seemed to have an inexplicable faith in me that I wasn't always able to muster myself.

I agreed, with one stipulation; no busy roads.

Though I had memorized the way from Champaign to the reserve base and from Champaign to Alan's house, being behind the wheel of a car changed everything. I'd had very little experience driving, and the thought of doing something wrong, of embarrassing myself in front of Jeff, put me in a panic. If I made a wrong move, I thought, all my flaws would suddenly be exposed. Intent on hiding my nervousness, I'd casually turn to him every few moments and ask, "Turn here?"

"Yep," He seemed extraordinarily calm, considering how inexperienced I was on the road.

"And here?"

"Yep."

Before I knew it, we had come to a four-way intersection.

"Turn left here," he said.

The volume of traffic going in that direction made my heart pound. In the rearview mirror, I could see other cars behind us and, as we waited for the light to change, I felt as if all eyes were on me.

Then it began to rain.

"No," I said suddenly. I no longer cared about impressing him or proving anything. "Forget it."

But Jeff looked unfazed. Mistaking his confidence for carelessness, I got angry.

"I told you no busy roads."

"But you're doing fine," he assured me gently.

Eventually, I came to love Jeff's calmness in the face of my anxiety, of what I interpreted as crisis. He seemed to have knowledge that I didn't: that everything would be "fine." But at that moment, I felt like keeping my foot firmly pressed on the brake pedal.

The light turned green. I didn't move.

Finally, Jeff reacted a bit more assertively. "Tina, you've got to go."

Daylight was fading. I imagined myself crashing into the line of cars next to me, ruining the image that I was trying so hard to maintain for him, and myself.

"When I say I don't want to do something—" I stopped. My tone had been harsher than I intended. Before I knew it, I was cruising along with the rest of the cars on a four-lane road with traffic going in both directions. My foot trembled against the gas pedal.

Jeff didn't say a word. He looked content to be sitting in the passenger seat. I was amazed.

After a while, we approached a hill. "Dammit," I said. The street was glistening with rain. Jeff seemed fine with that, too. He reminded me to maintain the same speed.

I slowed to a stop at a light, exhausted. I remembered driving with Millie, the way she would race with other drivers, changing lanes with relative ease while my heart leaped into my throat. I recalled swerving in and out of traffic on my bike, feeling as if nothing could compare with the kind of danger I lived through every day at home.

Suddenly, I was tired—weary of a lifetime of risks. Now, I just wanted to be safe. I wanted to be out of harm's way.

"You would have made the light," Jeff said kindly.

But I had had enough. I took a deep breath and looked at him. "Don't ever do that to me again."

He smiled at me and offered to drive the rest of the way. Though he took over, I'd gotten through the worst of it myself. I'd gone farther than I ever thought I could.

Chapter Seventeen

It Has a Name

In 1985, Susan took a semester off from college and went to live with her boyfriend in Springfield, Illinois. I felt lost in Champaign without her so, after completing my classes, I moved back to Alan's house.

I wasn't excited about the situation, but money was tight, and I had nowhere else to go. I put my plans for college on hold and began sending my résumé to local doctors' offices. Alan was charging me $350 a month for rent and, after two months, I ran out of funds. I saw what Susan had to go through—holding down several jobs at once and taking out loans to stay in school—and I just wasn't equal to the demands. The only alternative for me, it seemed, was to stay in the military and take advantage of its education benefits.

While I was staying with Alan and Nancy, I learned that Millie had returned from California. She, too, had run out of money and had no choice but to come back to live with her mother. Kathryn's new house was on the other side of Hinsdale, which she referred to as "Cardboard Heights." To Kathryn, the move was humbling, a big step down from what she was used to.

Susan had had to fly to California at least once during Millie's relatively brief stay there. Millie had been living with an aunt, Jackie, who called Susan one night, at her wits' end. What she described sounded like a psychotic episode; Millie had been screaming and threatening her.

"I love Millie," Aunt Jackie told Susan, "and I appreciate her driving out all this way to see us, but she has to go now." Susan got Millie on the telephone and gave her the name of a hotel to stay at until she could fly out and help her find a place. But six months later, Millie showed up back in Hinsdale, leaving behind unfinished college classes and an apartment full of new furniture.

By spring, Jeff had met nearly everyone in my family, but he had yet to meet my mother. During the eighteen months Millie was in California, I had no contact with her. When we finally spoke on the telephone, I sensed by the tone of her voice and her excitement in telling me stories of her travels that it would be a good time for her to meet Jeff.

The next morning, Jeff picked me up early to head to Chicago for a reserve meeting. Sinking into the seat of his car, I smiled at him, thinking, *now he'll run.*

"Jeff," I finally said, bracing myself, "it's time for you to meet my mother."

Jeff came from a big family. The Kotulskis were fun-loving, warm, and friendly and welcomed me as if I were their own daughter. They were nothing like my family.

By this time, Jeff had already learned a few things about us. He knew about Millie's suicide attempt, her hospitalizations, the trouble I had with her growing up. When Jeff met my father—who was delighted that I'd actually found a boyfriend—Alan took him aside and explained, privately, that because of Millie, because of my "genetics," there was a good chance that I could become "ill" at some point. He advised Jeff that "now would be a good time to leave."

Jeff told me about this conversation afterward, and I could see that he was embarrassed for both me and my father. Although he paid no attention to Alan, I was still mortified. There was no guarantee that Jeff wouldn't one day decide that my history was too much for him to bear. In order for him to understand the dynamics of my family, he had to know about my past. I had to give him the option of leaving before I fell too deeply in love with him.

Refusing to acquiesce to my father's bleak prophecy, I decided it was time. I owed it to myself to have someone who loved all of me. And, I figured, if Jeff could get past Millie after what Alan had said to him, the worst of it would be over.

"Sure," he answered cheerfully, agreeing to meet Millie.

Deep down, as much as I trusted Jeff's compassion and his acceptance of me, his response indicated he had no idea what I was asking him.

How to explain Millie. "She's different," I told him. "She has just done some very strange things." And Jeff simply nodded, as if to say, "Fine," as he did about so many things.

We headed to Kathryn's house. I prayed that Millie was in a good mood. As Jeff drove, I ran through in my head all the possible scenarios of how Millie might look, what she might say, what she might do.

We pulled into Kathryn's driveway just as Millie was walking out the front door.

"Yep," I said, "that's her."

She looked as if she were going to a beach party, wearing a sundress with large bright-orange flowers and big "Jackie O." sunglasses. It was late April. She had a deep tan, and her hair was streaked from the sun. I winced at her choice of clothing, but she looked as beautiful as always and even healthier than when I'd last seen her the year before. Long before she reached the car, she extended her hand in greeting. Slowly, deliberately, and loudly, she said, "Hello, Jeffrey." He must have thought she was hard of hearing because he greeted her with the same volume.

I let out the air I'd been holding in my chest; she was in a good mood. We ordered Chinese takeout that afternoon and ate lunch together at Kathryn's, chatting pleasantly about Jeff's work, Millie's adventures in California, and my classes. It was as if everything I'd told Jeff about my mother was made up. Afterward, as we were leaving, he looked at me. "Hey," he said, "that wasn't so bad."

Things fell together in ways I hadn't expected. Jeff had met my mother, and the visit had gone well. More importantly, he stuck around. I knew I was in love so, a little impulsively, I asked Jeff to marry me. I surprised even myself, but I was sure about how I felt. Jeff, however, didn't see the need to rush into things; he didn't think we were ready yet.

It felt like the first time in my life that I knew exactly what I wanted. I'd never been happier than I had been since meeting Jeff. But perhaps I was afraid to face the rejection of his gentle rebuff. Two weeks later, I signed up for active duty in Germany. Several months after I left, though, Jeff wrote to tell me he wished he had said yes.

While stationed in Würzburg, in southwestern Germany, I received several letters from Susan, Alan, and Nancy. Alan was very gracious while I was away, pleased I was doing something he strongly believed in: working at developing a trade for myself.

At one point, Alan wrote me about a letter he'd received from Susan in which she expressed serious concern about Millie's well-being. "Consider your mother *history*," he wrote. "If Susan wants to feel badly about her—let her. Susan did the best for her, and so did you. She needs maintenance not pity. Remember she still has a mother (Ms. Hall)." He also said he was proud of me and warned me not to try to help Susan, stating, "Let me deal with Susan's frustrations. I can afford it—man with big shoulders."

While Susan was still in Springfield, she moved Millie in with her. It wasn't a decision I agreed with, but I wasn't in a position to suggest another arrangement. Apparently, earlier on the very day that Jeff and I visited Millie, Millie had threatened Kathryn, insisting that she get "those people" to leave her alone. Millie then became aggressive, hitting Kathryn and breaking her glasses. When John came to Kathryn's and found out what had happened, he threw Millie to the floor.

The result was that Millie could no longer stay with Kathryn; she was just too volatile, too unpredictable. Susan tried to find her an apartment, but Millie had no money, and Kathryn could no longer help financially. Perhaps Susan felt it was easiest to take her in. But when, after several weeks, Millie woke Susan and her boyfriend in the middle of the night, shouting at imaginary people, Susan called the police. They took her to McFarland, a state-funded psychiatric hospital in Springfield.

The grounds for Millie's admission, according to the medical records, were that she was "delusional, yelling, suspicious—claimed 'they' were after her—claimed to be tormented by the radio and TV." While hospitalized, Millie was generally found "sitting at the periphery of unit activities smiling, aloof, and watchful."

> *She has been observed talking to herself and has made the following statements: "It's got nothing to do with me." "I've got a lover already." "I don't like that man across the street watching everything I do." Patient states that hospital is "two-faced." She made the statement that things were the best when she was married and raising her children and would like to be in that situation again.*

Apparently, though, Millie was refusing treatment and was not legally subject to involuntary admission. The attending physicians diagnosed her with schizoaffective disorder and discharged her because they judged that she wasn't a threat to herself or others and that she wasn't benefiting from hospitalization.

Millie told the doctors that she thought a car was circling the apartment where she lived and that Susan, in addition to "stealing" from her, was trying to "get inside her mind and control her." Despite these statements, the doctors wrote upon her discharge, "It is felt with minor supervision patient could maintain herself adequately and possibly get involved in some type of work or rehabilitation program."

One doctor wanted to perform a complete battery of tests that would have been helpful in establishing a definitive diagnosis. Unfortunately, however, Millie wasn't being "cooperative," so no tests were performed. The records suggest that her physicians had a plan for Millie upon discharge but, when she "refused all contact with mental health and local treatment providers," that too fell apart.

As Susan and I worked to try to help our mother establish herself, Millie's inability to understand that she was sick presented the greatest obstacle; in her mind, the difficulties that had marked her adult life had nothing to do with mental illness. Actually, it was her paranoia that prevented her from accepting help; she saw "strangers" and "authorities" as actively working to deprive her of freedom rather than helping her in any way.

To compound the difficulty of helping her get well, many of the medications Millie was alternately forced and asked to take had unwelcome side effects that were more evident to her than any benefits the drugs provided. This experience only reinforced her suspicions about the "true" motivations of her doctors.

This combination—Millie's status as an apparently competent adult, the laws protecting patients from unwanted treatment, and her inability to recognize her own disordered thinking—created a hellish merry-go-round for her and for us.

And so Millie's succession of unsuitable living arrangements and evictions began. The first apartment Millie moved into after her discharge from McFarland Hospital was crawling with roaches. With the help of her landlord, she moved to another place, but from there she was evicted. Apparently, the noise from the upstairs tenants exacerbated Millie's paranoia, and she began yelling at all hours.

Susan had moved to New York City to take acting and film-making classes but flew back home and helped Millie move to yet another place. This situation was stable for almost seven months. Then, one morning, while Millie was still in her bathrobe, the landlord and his two sons came into the apartment unannounced and started taking her belongings and putting them on the street. They took whatever cash she had for "back rent."

Millie lived on a busy street and, as the men dumped her things curbside, people pulled over, took what they wanted, and drove off. It was difficult to imagine what people could possibly want with family pictures, old clothes, and personal items, though there were a few valuable things—two antique tables from Kathryn's mother, a small Hummel collection, and some silver. But there was little Millie could do to stop them; it was mid-April and she was outside in her nightgown, grabbing what she could.

In the end, she was left with the clothes on her back and a plastic garbage bag filled with some salvaged odds and ends. Millie was forced to return to Kathryn's once again.

Susan wrote to me, "Mildred is pretty bad off. She's gotten kicked out of two apartments because of her continuous screaming battles with herself. I don't know what else I can do for her. I've done all I am capable of. She'll probably find another place in the Springfield area."

After only three weeks in Hinsdale, Millie got up in the middle of the night and grabbed Kathryn by the throat. Kathryn called the police; Millie, again, was on her own.

Shortly after that, I came home on leave from Germany. When I finally talked with Susan, after receiving her letters and updates, I couldn't hold back. I discovered that Susan was just as upset as I was, but I couldn't help blaming her for allowing Millie to be in so much danger.

"She needed help," I told Susan, as if it weren't already obvious. "You can't just move her somewhere and take off."

In the end, we both broke down in tears.

I thought Millie should have been near Kathryn all along, in the neighborhood she was accustomed to, with family nearby. Susan felt this was too expensive, so she found apartments outside of town, but in places where no one knew Millie.

Of course, Susan had Millie's best interests in mind, and she was trying to do everything she could to keep her off the street, but Susan lacked sufficient resources. She also, at times, tried to ignore Millie's psychotic episodes. "Mom," she would tell her, "you're going to be fine. You just need a nice place of your own." But our mother actually needed medication and a structured, supervised environment.

In the coming years, Susan and I seemed to be forever at odds about how to handle Millie. Alan and Nancy would have nothing to do with Millie's affairs, and Kathryn was advancing in age and unable to help as much as she used to.

Also, Millie's stepbrother Wes, who had been an advocate for her both during her divorce and in her medical treatment, was gone; he had committed suicide by shooting himself in the head. He'd struggled with alcoholism for many years and had sunk into a deep depression. Millie didn't hear about his suicide until much later. On the last night of his life in November 1983, he left behind only a quote from Act 5, Scene 2 of *Hamlet:* "There's a divinity that shapes our ends, Rough hew them though we may."

Eventually, Susan had had enough as well. She wrote, "For many years actually, I felt I needed to get away from the family and their criticism. Of course, I'm really not away from them at all. No matter where I am, I feel tormented by the whole situation. I don't know if things will ever be better. God, I pray that they will, though."

While I was still on leave from Germany, Jeff and I had planned to elope on his birthday and then have a big wedding on my birthday a year later; the idea was that we were going to be lifelong birthday presents to each other. But the night before we were to marry, we confessed to Alan and Nancy. Despite everything, I wanted their blessing and, before we knew it, they were arranging a ceremony for us. They discouraged us from getting married by a justice of the peace, insisting we have a proper wedding in their home. Their gesture took me by surprise; perhaps they were delighted to see me finally on my own.

Nancy called a pastor, a pianist, and a caterer. The next morning, she took me dress shopping. We walked into a nearby bridal shop and Nancy said, "This girl needs a wedding dress." The seamstress took out a clipboard and asked for the date of the wedding. When Nancy replied, "Today," the seamstress's eyes grew big and she called out, "Mrs. Rutherford!" A pleasant woman appeared and showed us seven wedding dresses. I picked one, got measured, and came back later that day to pick it up.

Meanwhile, Jeff went to rent a tuxedo. Then later, back at the house, Alan offered to pay for our honeymoon. "Anywhere you guys want to go," Alan said. Jeff, humble as always, didn't respond at first. After a few moments, Alan said again, "Anywhere," and Jeff replied, "Well, I've been to Wisconsin."

For all the fuss Alan and Nancy made over Jeff and me, I feared that I might cause a major problem. I wanted Millie to be present at our wedding, but I worried about bringing her into Alan and Nancy's home. At the last minute, concerned I'd hurt my mother by leaving her out, I decided to call her but discovered she didn't have a telephone in her new apartment.

At six o'clock that evening, without my mother present, Jeff and I were married.

I had to return to Germany shortly afterward but was discharged just six months later due to a serious blood clot in my leg. In any case, I was just happy to go home to Jeff.

He'd finished his coursework and was planning to begin medical school in the fall. We lived, briefly, at Alan and Nancy's guesthouse until we found a place of our own. While Jeff studied around the clock, I worked at a Veterans Administration hospital across the street from Madden Zone Center where, Kathryn informed us, Millie had been hospitalized again.

According to Millie's medical records, "She had been homeless and wandering the streets for about three weeks. She was acting bizarre, delusional, screaming at imaginary people as loudly as possible, and acting out violently toward people not present, and she was armed with a butcher knife to protect herself from people." Without any of us knowing, Millie had once again been evicted, living in her car until it was impounded. Susan had been contacted by the owner of the impound lot where Millie's car had been towed.

We drove to the impound lot and paid $300 to retrieve the car. The owner said he felt bad about what had happened, referring to Millie as the "homeless woman." He told us her car had been there for several months.

When Jeff and I drove Millie's car back to Kathryn's, we noticed that it was running poorly. Jeff's father, who knew something about auto mechanics, said he'd take a look at it. When he took off a wheel to inspect the brakes, he found a corncob tucked inside. He tossed it at us and joked, "Start the grill."

The staff at Madden explained that they couldn't tell us what had happened, whether Millie had been given medications, or what condition she was in. We didn't have legal guardianship over her and were therefore not privy to confidential information about Millie.

Susan was able to obtain some information about our mother, but very little. A therapist had written in Millie's medical records, "Patient seemed immature when expressed plans for getting out of the hospital and needing a man to help her get an apartment and to look over her. She was attached to a young male patient and talked about moving in with him after discharge."

Yet, without Millie's consent, there was nothing the therapist could do for her. When asked how she would like to proceed, Millie said she "felt rejected and that she could not live with her mother until she was able to get herself back on her feet."

Before Susan returned to New York, she called me. Millie's diagnosis had been suddenly changed. When Jeff and I arrived at the hospital, we still weren't allowed to see Millie, but Susan came out to meet us. She looked to me, at that moment, much older than her years.

"They told me that Millie has paranoid schizophrenia," she said. "It's one of the worst cases they've seen. Mom," she added, "is very, very sick."

It finally had a name.

Chapter Eighteen

Making Sense of the Past

For me, naming Millie's illness was a great relief. It helped make sense of the past twenty years of our lives. But with the diagnosis, grief, mourning, and anger also came.

I was angry with the innumerable people who'd come in and out of our lives, who'd encountered Millie—especially the doctors and our closest relatives, including Alan. How different things could have been had someone stepped in sooner—ten years earlier, five even.

In the end, as I traced the silhouette that had finally emerged from the darkness, I also blamed myself. It had taken shape, after all these years, and I wondered: *Was there a moment when it was clear to me, when I myself had looked away?*

All our lives, we'd been at the mercy of an illness that had a name. We just hadn't known it. And no one else had recognized it, even those who really should have.

But in the days following the diagnosis, there was little time to worry about taking blame, and there were actually fewer questions than I'd expected. Yet I also carried around a kind of humiliation. Doctors knew the name of my mother's tormentor, but not what it had cost us.

Why didn't you do something sooner? said a voice in my head. But eventually, as we worked to stabilize Millie and regroup in the aftermath of the earthquake we'd endured, the guilt began to fade. It was then replaced by a terrible grief.

Millie was in Madden for nearly seven months.

In June, Susan wrote, "This letter is to inform you of the continuing saga of Millie the miserable." Susan had taken Millie to three group homes, but Millie became angry and hostile in each. Shortly afterward, Susan said she had finally found Clayton House in Lincoln Park, Chicago, a large rooming house that provided three daily meals, counseling, and supervised administration of medication. Residents were free to come and go as they pleased, though there was a curfew. The program seemed a perfect match for Millie.

But after Millie had been there for a few weeks, Jeff and I went to visit her, and I was shocked at the situation. Clayton House was, in fact, a halfway house—a drug rehabilitation center for the urban poor. A drab brick building with bars on the windows, it was frequently patrolled by police, which only served to heighten Millie's paranoia. The place wasn't visibly dirty, but I got the sense that it was never cleaned thoroughly. The elevator smelled of urine, and the walls were yellowed from cigarette smoke.

We took Millie to lunch, and she seemed in good spirits, apparently unaware of or unconcerned by the repugnance of her surroundings. After we left her, I sobbed. When I got home, I started making calls to find a better solution. During that time, I received two letters from Millie. In one, she wrote about how good she had had it in California; in the other, she seemed perfectly upbeat and optimistic:

Dear Tina,

I'll have to get over to your apartment once I leave here. It'll probably take a month or two to find a job. Have you started work yet? Working can be nice. Grandma Smiley and Grams never had to work—just at home. That can be nice to. [sic] I really miss cooking. Can't wait to cook again.

I'll have you over. How's school Jeff? Is your full name Jeffrey. I should be addressing the envelope more properly.

Isn't this nice weather. Except the day you came in. It was a major trip for Kathryn. She did well though. The people here certainly raved about your beauty. You have a very nice looking husband too. Tina, are you happy. I liked married life and miss it sometimes. Susan would like to get married soon and have a couple of kids. She's 24 now—hard to believe how time flies. I love kids too.

Well see you soon. Take care of yourselves.
Love, Millie ox

After some investigation, I found Millie an apartment in Downers Grove. While it wasn't the nicest place, we were able to negotiate a reduced rent. Millie began working at a hardware store. However, the job didn't last long; she was fired because she wasn't fast enough on the cash register.

Millie soon got another job, this time at a fabric store. Between her wages, public assistance, and Social Security, she managed to get by. She spent six relatively normal months in that apartment, and Susan and I lived by the motto "no news is good news."

During that time, the summer after Jeff's first year in medical school, I learned I was pregnant. Jeff and I hadn't planned on starting a family so soon; in fact, in our frequent conversations about children, I had told Jeff I didn't want any. Our official plan was for me to work to help Jeff through medical school. But in fact, I was terrified at the thought of having my own children.

Susan and I were just beginning to learn the inner workings of the state mental health system, which seemed designed to protect everyone but Millie. As long as Millie wasn't judged "a threat to herself or others," by standards that I could never understand, she was on her own. Because Susan and I didn't have legal guardianship of our mother, we had virtually no influence on, or even information about, the course of Millie's treatment.

As a result, Millie became a "revolving-door patient," a person whose illness and treatment followed a repeating and tragic cycle. Typically, when she was discharged from a hospital, she would stop taking her medication, which resulted in a psychotic episode. Eventually, her condition would deteriorate to a point at which those around her got scared or complained. The police then intervened, and she was returned to a hospital. Once stabilized, she was deemed "not dangerous" and was again discharged, almost always without our knowledge, to do as she pleased—starting yet another turn in the endlessly rotating cycle. If Millie didn't want to live in a group home, fine. If she chose not to take medication, that was her prerogative. This is why the system becomes tremendously frustrating for family members; we simply had no say, no power to stop the cycle from repeating.

No hospital could share information about our mother with Susan and me unless Millie signed a release. There were times when we lost track of Millie completely, and hospital receptionists weren't even permitted to tell us whether she had been admitted. And when Millie was sick, she wanted nothing to do with signing forms, taking medication, or complying with anything doctors told her to do. Most times, these requests would feed into her delusions. She feared that signing a form meant she was giving up any hope of freedom.

The one consistent thing about Millie's medical care up to this point was its inconsistency. In Illinois, medical records for the mentally ill were not transferred between counties, and Millie managed to tour the state. If she had been hospitalized previously in DuPage County, a hospital in Cook County would have no record of it. Accurately assessing a patient with such a complicated history—and Millie was hardly a reliable narrator, especially when involuntarily admitted—was impossible. Each time she entered a different hospital, Millie's illness was simply treated anew; new doctor, new medications, new diagnoses, and no clear sense of the cycles and patterns of her past behavior. Without that insight, her treatment went nowhere.

Had Millie's care been more consistent, a definitive diagnosis been determined sooner, and her post-hospital placements stable and supervised, she might have been less of a burden. But she was never provided with any real resources, education, or understanding of her illness and its implications. Families dealing with a mentally ill family member often give up, or come very close to doing so; hence the number of homeless patients with nowhere to go.

Although Susan and I were not permitted much involvement in our mother's care, we did everything we could to keep her stable. Unfortunately, her apartment stays ended in evictions, her hospital stays with new medications and new side effects. Susan and I were sucked into a maelstrom of despair, right along with Millie.

I spent years learning how to set and maintain boundaries with my mother, how not to be a mother to her and, most of all, how to find my own identity through my faith and marriage. Unlike previously, sometimes I was simply loath to get involved. Millie was very depressing to be around when she was noncompliant, when she believed everyone, including the doctors, was out to kill her. Yet, the thought of where she might end up without help from Susan and me continued to haunt me, so I kept trying.

Eventually, I had to move Millie out of her apartment in Downers Grove. One night she called me, shivering through clenched teeth.

When I arrived, her apartment was flooded, and she was without heat. She had stopped paying rent and was too terrified to open her door when the landlord came banging on it.

In the later months of my pregnancy, the days grew longer because Jeff spent more time at school, and I was forced to confront my own impending motherhood.

Being a caretaker gave me a sense of purpose. I did all I could to support Jeff in his career—working long hours to minimize student loans, quizzing him, encouraging him, perhaps even living his education vicariously. I clipped coupons, watched our budget; I cooked and cleaned and worked full-time throughout my pregnancy. Kathryn was becoming more infirm and less independent, so I helped her with errands. Millie, of course, was a full-time job by herself. In doing so much for everyone else, I was able to lose myself, to avoid thinking about what *I* wanted. Inevitably, that meant my own needs came last.

I didn't talk with Jeff about my fears of raising a child. I worried that if I did, he might begin to question my capacity to be a good mother. In the evenings, he began reading to me from his medical books. At one point, he was studying childhood development.

"Children who are spanked and ridiculed as a form of discipline," he told me one night, "are more likely to have emotional scars."

"Well, that's pretty obvious," I snapped. I was getting sick of these nightly readings, tired of Jeff's telling me things I already knew from experience. "What are you trying to say?"

Jeff patiently explained that experts in their fields wrote these books, and that we both could benefit from learning more. I wasn't convinced, and Nancy's old prophecy returned to me, again and again: I'd grow up, get divorced, and end up beating my children.

Jeff's education and a baby on the way represented a fresh start for me, yet I was still carrying a great deal of baggage: Millie's evictions and hospitalizations, Kathryn's slow decline, and the incessant disagreements with Susan about our mother's care. I was starting over with a new family, determined not to make the same mistakes as others; I refused to let anything ruin my progress. What I needed, more than anything else, was for my family to start pulling its own weight so I could have enough room to care for myself and build my new life.

When Jeff came home with his medical books, telling me what he'd just learned about mental illness, about family members of the mentally ill, I cringed. I wanted to tell him to shut up about his books, to remind him that I'd been through it all firsthand, not via some professor's lectures. His information sessions with me were well-meaning, but I began to fear he was losing faith in me.

Jeff had had what seemed to me a perfect childhood—a wonderful family, many accomplishments, and an ability to continually look at the bright side. He'd always been laid back and non-confrontational. But between advocating for Millie, facing Alan's continuing criticism of me, and contending with Susan's perspective, I was constantly hardening myself so I could stand up to everyone.

Sometimes, Jeff would say, "Tina, why can't you just be happy?" Of course, when he said this, I wanted to slug him, though he never meant it snidely or dismissively. He just wanted me to feel good about things for a change but, instead, I began to resent him, and that troubled me greatly.

Sometimes, I found myself simply wanting to say to him, *You have no idea what it's like.* Jeff's family problems and issues were usually resolved reasonably; my family's never were. Because I couldn't put an end to the dysfunction of my own family, I worried that Jeff would see this as a failing, a persistent flaw, eclipsing anything else I did. He quoted statistics, case histories, results of new research. I thought my own husband was scrutinizing me, as if he were using my background as a test project, waiting for me to crumble, to prove his theories. I began to feel estranged from him, to put more distance between us, insisting that he could never understand. I was on a mission to prove him wrong.

Though I jogged throughout my first trimester and walked regularly during the rest of my pregnancy, I put on more weight than normal, according to my obstetrician. Because of my dealings with family members, the estrangement I felt from Jeff, and the loneliness I felt during the long days Jeff spent at school, I began to eat as a way to soothe my emotions. One of the new comforts Susan and I had as children was chocolate. Millie's pots of fudge were like a salve, and I associated them with pleasure. Carrying that association into my adult years, I grabbed chocolate whenever things felt out of control.

As my feelings of abandonment increased, so did my cravings for chocolate. And with them came physical ailments—acne, irregular sleeping habits, hair loss, and bouts of depression. Though some of it was hormonal in origin, there was an aspect of it that I could no longer ignore. My weight gain, regardless of my pregnancy, seemed to be a blinking red light calling for my immediate attention. I'd been hiding it all, stuffing it down with chocolate and junk food, unwilling to look back at my past to connect it with my present, afraid that, in doing so, I would somehow empower it to take control of me. It took a long time for me to realize that my husband wasn't my enemy, that I avoided confronting my past because of an insistence on perfection, and that I had been refusing to accept what I knew in my heart to be true. I wanted so much to believe that I had survived, that I was on the mend. But the truth was that I still had a long way to go.

On March 13, 1989, our son Charles was born. I was delighted and relieved; Jeff was as proud as could be. And our lives promptly reached a new level of havoc we had never expected.

Charles had colic, and Jeff began his clinical rotations,working thirty-six-hour shifts. For all the fighting Jeff and I had done about parenting during my pregnancy, we did maintain a sort of dreamy idealism about having a child. With Charles on the scene, however, there was no time for arguing, let alone dreaminess. When I left the room for even a moment, Charles screamed. It was the sound of something inhuman, perhaps extraterrestrial. I held him and rocked him and kept him in motion around the clock; his crying seemed like a siren with no off switch. Jeff slept every few days, and I have little recollection of whether I slept or not. We became zombies, barely able to mouth words to one another, passing each other, exhausted and disheveled, at hours when the rest of the world had the luxury of dreaming.

When Charles was less than a month old, Alan came to visit, unexpectedly, with a coworker of his. During that time, I couldn't be bothered with combing my hair, and it wasn't uncommon for me to continue wearing the same clothes I'd worn to bed the night before.

Alan looked around at the apartment in shambles and shook his head. "You're just like your mother," he declared, and left. His coworker, a bit red in the face, lingered for a moment, smiling and telling me what a beautiful baby I had, and then followed Alan out the door.

After Susan was born, Millie had tried to slit her own wrists. Would this be my fate, too? Was that what my father was referring to? After he left that day, a wave of depression seemed to cast a pall over my screaming child and me. What if this was the start of something? Why did my baby cry so much? The questions lingered and festered.

My doctor urged me to get some family support. I was sleep-deprived and at my wits' end. "Things will get better once you get some sleep," he told me. But family support and money for child-care were two things we didn't have. Jeff's mother had multiple sclerosis, his father had had six heart attacks; we simply couldn't expose them to the stress of a constantly wailing baby. Jeff's sisters worked full-time, and I refused to trust a stranger with my newborn. This was my baby, my responsibility; sleep or no sleep, I was determined to do everything I could to be a good mother.

In later months, as Charles' colic subsided and I caught up on sleep, I felt some of my old stubbornness and strength return to me. Like an anonymous gift left at my door, I couldn't explain where it had come from, but I accepted it and held on to it. I began to find the space and time to look at my past and to seek answers. Millie, I slowly and painfully came to understand, had hurt me because she was very ill, and it was *this illness* that had caused us so much hell, not Millie herself.

Still, Millie was afflicted by something that people were ashamed of; its stigma carried a huge weight. I became upset at the people around her who ignored or were frightened by her diagnosis. Glossing over the issues surrounding her illness would not help Millie; that only served to make her invisible. But I began to trust in letting others come to terms with her illness in their own time.

Understanding Millie's illness allowed me to forgive her for her atrocities. She had stuck by me as best she could and, no matter what, I couldn't turn my back on her and let her end up on the street. I started dealing with my anger—the anger that gathered in me like a hurricane. I had no excuses for not helping her; no one did.

What I had to accept was that Millie's illness was never going away; she simply could not live on her own, and she would always be dependent on us. Knowing Millie also meant having to accept the often-frightening manifestations of her illness. But beneath that, she was still my mother: vulnerable, charming, witty, beautiful, and kind.

Eventually, I began telling everyone that my mother has paranoid schizophrenia. I gave people the option to step back, ask questions, or walk away, but I would no longer deny that Millie was a part of me. I wasn't ashamed of her, and that acceptance seemed to reflect in my child's becoming well; he had finally begun opening his mouth to smile rather than to scream. To me, this was a gift of grace.

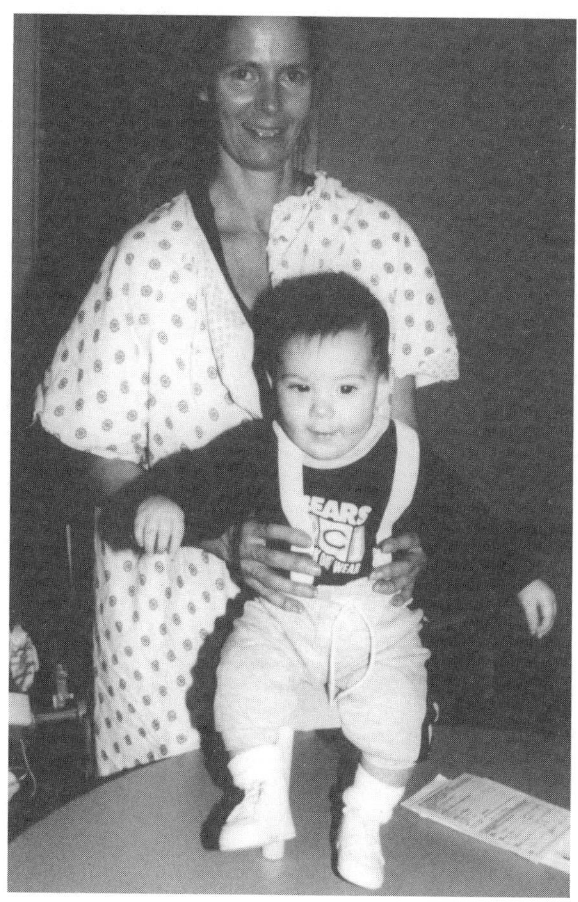

Grandma Millie and Charles

Chapter Nineteen

My Mother's Keeper

While I was still pregnant with Charles, my mother's cousin Nancy called. She said that the Downers Grove police had received several complaints about Millie, whose fellow tenants—though very apologetic—were concerned that she might be keeping wild animals in her unit. She'd also been yelling profanities at construction workers repaving the road.

When I got to Millie's apartment, Nancy was just about to leave, since my mother wouldn't let her in. Millie kept me outside for a long time too as I tried to convince her to open the door.

Finally, Nancy left, and Millie opened the door, telephone to her ear. Her belongings were still piled in big black garbage bags, untouched since she had moved in six months prior. For furniture, she had only a kitchen set and a recliner that Jeff and I had given her. I felt a wave of guilt for not coming by sooner to help her unpack. I realized that, as busy as I'd been preparing for the baby, I'd also been staying away deliberately, sorting through my own feelings.

When Millie hung up the telephone, she collapsed into a seat at the kitchen table.

"C'mon, Mom," I said. "Let's go get some lunch."

It occurred to me that if Millie wasn't paying rent, she likely wasn't paying her telephone bill, either. When she turned to get her things, I picked up the receiver. There was no dial tone; the plug wasn't even connected to the wall jack.

I drove my mother straight to Good Samaritan Hospital, but Millie refused to sign the release form, which meant that I had no access to information about her care. Then, just a few days later, she was discharged. Millie's doctors said afterwards they had found no reason to keep her as an inpatient.

One of the toughest things for family members of the mentally ill is deciding to have them committed. It can feel like an act of utter betrayal. Of course, from long experience, I knew when hospitalization was best for everyone. But no matter how many times I had to intervene and cart my mother off to the nearest hospital, that guilt haunted me.

In the days and months after she was diagnosed with paranoid schizophrenia, Millie was particularly difficult. The barrage of doctor's appointments, neurological tests, and new medications only served to heighten her distrust. I think, beyond anything else, Millie was afraid of being abandoned, afraid that none of us would accept her illness. In fact, she used to tell Jeff—but never me—when she would hear voices. Perhaps my candor, my refusal to treat her as a victim, made her more cautious around me.

But however blunt I was with Millie and whatever limits I set on her behavior, I still never had enough armor to be fully protected. At times, she was excruciatingly critical—I was gaining too much weight, my hair wasn't right, I had no right to be angry. I began to understand that she had chosen me as an outlet for her rage, so I started preparing myself before each time I saw her. Though I reacted to her sniping less often, it never became any less painful.

Other family members had their own ways of coping with her. Kathryn, worried that she had somehow damaged her daughter, was often incapable of helping Millie. However, she'd gently remind Susan and me that our mother needed us, and she was able to support us in caring for Millie. By doing this, I believe she felt she could achieve a measure of atonement.

Other than Millie, Susan and I were the ones most affected by the diagnosis; our entire lives had to change to accommodate it. Who else would be her keepers? Millie needed constant monitoring, advocacy, and supervision. A common stereotype of people suffering from mental illness is that they are consigned to mental wards for the remainder of their days, living in relative comfort, free from the demands of work, weaving baskets and shuffling around in hospital gowns. Another familiar belief is that they lead normal lives through medication.

The truth for many people suffering from mental illness is that they are unable to get the support and guidance they need through the system itself, from the professionals who work with them. Without family, they'd very likely end up on the street.

Late one night before Christmas, Millie's brother John telephoned me unexpectedly; I think it was the first time he'd ever actually called me. He sounded nervous and hesitant, and he'd clearly been drinking. I asked him what was wrong.

John started to talk about his father and how Kathryn had hidden everything from him and Millie.

"I had no idea he was dying," he said. "No one ever said anything. I never got to say good-bye to my own father."

John said that he avoided Kathryn after his father's death; his relationship with his sister also soured then. Like Millie, he felt his needs were never met and that, regardless of his mother's material provision, he'd always been on his own.

What struck me, though, was his compassion for his sister; previously, I'd never seen much evidence that he cared for her. All along, he'd had a deep understanding of Millie, a shared sense of loss with her. But he'd always been too caught up in his own pain and resentment to discuss his feelings or help support Millie. Only after he'd realized that his sister was very sick was he able to forgive.

After Millie's last eviction, a county social worker met with Susan and recommended that we look into YMCA locations for vacancies. Luckily for us, someone had just moved out of the Y in LaGrange, Illinois, and Millie was able to rent a single room at the end of a hallway on the second floor.

While Millie lived at the Y for several years, I worked to make a safe and predictable home for my young family. Unquestionably, my priorities had changed somewhat. For this reason, I may not have responded as quickly to Millie's anxiety and paranoia as I had in the past, but I still kept in close contact with her via our weekly conversations.

I took Millie out when I could, and this always seemed to help her feel better. Living at the Y depressed Millie, and simply getting out for a while improved her mood. Even more significantly, spending time with my children had a positive effect on her that no medication could equal. Millie adored her grandchildren and, as stressful as it was then to orchestrate an outing, I tried to get them together as often as possible.

One of the many trips to the zoo.
Left to Right. Millie, Eddie, Sarah (cousin), Charles and Amy (cousin)

A few years after my second son, Eddie, was born, I arranged to take my mother and the boys on a trip to a zoo. That morning we quickly got off on the wrong foot. My boys were antsy and excited in the backseat and, as soon as Millie got into the car, she was ranting about the bathrooms on her floor, which she had to share with twenty other women. Through the rearview mirror, I could see my sons react to the tension Millie brought into the car, and I could sense that she had gone off her medication.

"Mom," I said, trying to hide my anger and hoping to change the subject, "we're really excited about the zoo today."

She was sitting forward in her seat, so I asked her to sit back, but she ignored me, remaining tense and upright. I immediately regretted putting my children in this situation—the very one I'd lived as a child. I was terrified of having them hear the voice of their grandmother's illness.

Almost without thinking, I made a decision. I put my turn signal on and circled back around in the direction of the Y. Then I pulled over at the edge of the parking lot, reached across Millie's lap, and opened her door.

"What are you doing?" Millie asked with panic on her face.

Sharply, I replied, "You need to get out."

The boys became quiet, and I sat back, leaving the door open at Millie's side. As my heart pounded in my chest, I continued looking at her, showing my resolve. I knew she had been looking forward to this trip; we had been planning it for a while. I knew, too, that on some level, she couldn't help herself, but there wasn't anything I could do at the moment to stop her from having an episode. My only concern at that moment was to get her out of the car before her inability to stay composed frightened the boys.

She held on to the door handle and looked back at me, puzzled.

"Why are you doing this?" she asked, slumping over in her seat, her eyes pleading as if she were begging me not to force her back out into the world of strangers.

I wanted so much for her to be happy, to feel safe. But now I was a mother; I felt torn between protecting my children from her delusions and protecting my mother from herself. I reminded her, gently, about our deal: If she didn't take her medication, she couldn't see the boys.

She hadn't realized how she was acting. Turning toward me to say good-bye, she said, "All better now." But I knew it didn't work that way with Millie, and I promised to get together another time soon.

I waited to make sure she got back inside her building. After she disappeared through the door, I drove off.

When my father visited me after the birth of my first child, I was just beginning to deal with the challenges of mothering a baby who was plagued with never-ending colic. His scornful words stung me to the core. Had I listened to him, perhaps my family's life might have turned out differently. Had I given in to my fears of becoming like my mother, I might have sacrificed my chance to be a good mother to my own children, and the cycle of abuse would have continued. What has taken me years to realize is that Millie's illness is not my own.

Whether out of empathy, fear, or a combination of both, I see the signs. There are times when I feel as if I'm always on guard. When my children bound into the room, unexpectedly, I jump—nothing too unusual, of course—but then find myself recalling how I used to frighten Millie when she was in a daze in front of the television. It seems odd to have to reassure myself that I'm not showing symptoms of paranoia but only reacting normally to everyday life. Sometimes, however, I can't tell the difference; a part of me is always monitoring my behavior, looking for signs of irrationality.

But I have been fortunate. I do not have paranoid schizophrenia, and the chances of my developing it at this stage in life are next to none. What has helped more than anything else is simple compassion toward Millie; without it, I find myself feeling guilt, pity, and estrangement.

Sometimes, I feel so pained by Millie's suffering that I imagine taking some of it away from her, but I give myself permission only to empathize and limit it to that. Otherwise, I would open myself to other emotions that would prevent me from having any kind of relationship with her. It has taken me a long time to appreciate that I have been given an opportunity—free of mental illness—to be a mother to my children, and I can do that without guilt. Only through a deeper understanding of Millie and the acceptance of her illness in our lives could I find ways to mend some of the fractures of the past.

A few years ago, Alan and Nancy came to visit me at my home in Minnesota. I was worried that they'd think my house was messy or that I wasn't a good enough mother. But as they concluded their visit, they each said to me how impressed they were by the home I'd created for my family.

Of course, there are days when I feel like I'm at the center of a three-ring circus, when my kids are putting me to every possible test. But I find that the values I have instilled in my children are reflected back to me. My children remind me how to laugh things off, how to embrace a new day, and how to accept and forgive.

This hasn't been as easy with Millie. Setting limits with her required a sort of tough love that could sometimes break my heart. But the reversal of roles, with me reminding her of rules and holding her accountable for violating them, has enabled her to be a real part of our family. Her grandchildren have given her another chance. They adore her and look forward to spending time with her. Seeing my mother's face light up when they're around and how she laughs with them has been a small miracle in itself.

Because Millie didn't recognize the seriousness of stopping her medication, I made deals with her. These were limits that both she and I could benefit from; I knew she was capable of taking her medicine consistently, so I refused to cater to her when she didn't. I provided Millie with consequences that were tangible to her; canceling outings and not allowing her to see the kids.

Many people suffering from schizophrenia (and other serious mental disorders) fail to see the need for their medication, so often they stop taking it, unaware of the dangers of noncompliance. An additional risk for Millie was that she would be threatened with eviction from the Y if she didn't take her medicine.

I had to earn Millie's trust—it was the only way I could truly act as her advocate—and empathize with her reluctance to take medications that had undesirable side effects. At the same time, however, I knew that if she refused treatment, the outcome for her would be far worse. I was unwilling to take the chance that she could make it on her own without support and guidance.

Eventually, I was able to develop a dialogue with the manager at the Y. She agreed to call me first if she noticed Millie behaving oddly—which Millie often did, usually yelling—and I agreed to do my best to work with my mother before she put herself in danger of eviction.

However, due to the laws governing the state mental health system, I still had no access to Millie's doctors or medical records. I couldn't sit in on any meetings or even get a message to Millie's caseworker at Family Services, where she was supposed to go for monthly appointments. Several times, these "caregivers" actually hung up on me. If they behaved this way with me, I wondered, how must they be treating Millie?

I knew, of course, that I couldn't leave it all up to Millie, and some days I resented my mother for this. Sometimes, she got angry with me for holding her accountable; sometimes, she just wanted to be enraged without consequences. And often, Millie could be like a child, taking advantage of any slack I gave her. But giving her clear limits provided her with a sense of safety. Being consistent and holding her responsible was, in the end, actually the best way to deal with her; it was also the easiest and fairest for my family and me. Regardless of whether she showed it, Millie knew that I wouldn't let anything terrible happen to her if I could prevent it.

Being Millie's advocate has hardened me. Talking with doctors, insisting that Millie get the kind of treatment—be it medication or respect—that she deserves, and expressing my frustration with careless doctors and nurses hasn't been easy. I've often regretted the fact that I can't be soft. A friend once told me that I am intense at times, that I have a difficult time letting go of control. I know that she was right.

My sense of safety can still be frighteningly fragile, and certain situations set me off. Navigating the New York City subway system is one; getting lost while driving is another. For example, my husband isn't great with directions; when he loses his way, my old feelings of vulnerability creep in again. I'll immediately start to feel anxious, sometimes disproportionately so. I've sometimes wanted Jeff to take control so I can relax more, but I also have a hard time letting go of the reins. And as an adult daughter, I must constantly relearn how to be a child, free-spirited and loved. Otherwise, my protective wall goes up.

In failing to interrupt old patterns and learned behaviors, in repeating the cycles of abuse and shame, people can unwittingly sabotage not only their chance to be loved but also their chance at happiness. Though there are times when I would like to run off and forget everything, acknowledging that my mother's illness is not going away and accepting things as they are has actually freed me to have the life I want.

Chapter Twenty

The End of the Line

One night when Jeff and I were driving to the Twin Cities, we heard on the radio that the YMCA in LaGrange, Illinois (where Millie was living), was on fire. Eighteen fire departments responded to the blaze; seven people were injured, and one was killed. The Red Cross got involved and was apparently moving displaced residents to a nearby motel. Since we were several hours away, I called John for help.

John found the motel that Millie had been moved to. When I called, the owner, likely overwhelmed, abruptly hung up on me. However, John was able to get through to Millie and talk with her. He assured me she was safe but told me she kept saying, "Get me out of here."

John volunteered to have Millie come live with him until her situation got settled. Although I worried that, frightened and alone and without her medication, Millie would be on the verge of psychosis, John met Millie at the motel and brought her back home with him.

When I arrived a couple days later, Millie was visibly shaken. I reassured her that I would salvage what I could from her room.

Most of Millie's things were smoke-damaged, but she was adamant about keeping everything, so I took clothes and other washables to a local self-service laundry.

Fortunately, we were able to quickly get Millie situated with her medications and belongings. She told me she felt relieved that she wasn't injured but reported having nightmares about being trapped in a fire for months afterward.

Before long, Millie overstayed her welcome at John's. She'd been staying up all night, and John admitted to me that he didn't trust her, that he was having trouble sleeping. So, we moved her into a motel and then into a supervised apartment. However, one night, she went to a local emergency room and reported to the intake staff that she felt afraid and could no longer care for herself. It was the first time Millie had ever admitted her fears to a hospital staff.

Susan and I were increasingly aware that our mother's precarious living situations would continue to fall apart. We needed to arrange something more permanent and stable, which wasn't easy in Illinois. There were long waiting lists for group homes. What's more, placement involved lengthy interviews, health assessments, and medication compliance—never a strong suit for Millie.

Around this time, Kathryn was becoming too feeble to be self-sufficient. John hired a series of aides to provide home health care, but Kathryn proved too hostile for anyone to work with. John, Susan, and I explained to her repeatedly that she could avoid a nursing home only if she were kinder to the women trying to help her, but to no avail. Finally, Kathryn went to live in a nursing home. After several years there, she seemed to lose her will to live.

I knew it broke Millie's heart to see her mother getting older. She visited Kathryn each day, walking the two miles from her supervised apartment. Being in the nursing home and seeing her mother there made her deeply upset. Still, Millie tried to comfort Kathryn.

"It's not your fault your face broke out," she told her mother gently. "It's drugs and germs, and it's happening to everyone—even Elizabeth Taylor."

The stress of Kathryn's situation eventually took its toll on Millie. Susan had just begun bringing her camera around, toying with the idea of making a film about our mother's illness and her battle with the public health system. Kathryn's placement in the nursing home evoked deep-seated resentment in Millie, and with that came psychotic episodes, one of which Susan caught on film.

At the time, Millie was enraged to hear that one of Kathryn's doctors wanted to treat Kathryn with antidepressants. Clearly, it triggered Millie's distrust of doctors, her feelings of victimization by the system, and her sense of helplessness.

"He's a way-out-of-line hotshot," she said. "This whole goddamn state is disgusting. This whole goddamn country is disgusting. I'm not going to end up like that. People are the most disgusting things on the face of the earth."

Only a few weeks after Millie's tirade, Kathryn died.

Millie's problems with living arrangements replayed over and over. She'd already been in and out of seventeen psychiatric wards, eight apartments, three boarding houses, and countless motels. I no longer tried to give her hope that she could ever again live on her own.

"I think it's my age," Millie once told a caseworker, explaining why she didn't like living the way she did. "I'm just very sensitive about being in this immature position." She wanted what everyone else around her had: a job, a relationship, and independence.

Susan and I often differed on what we believed Millie was capable of accomplishing. We both ultimately wanted the same thing for our mother, but Susan had a hard time accepting the fact that Millie couldn't live on her own.

I knew that many of the medications Millie had taken over the years had provided undesirable side effects, but I also believed that Millie had an illness that could be controlled only with medication. Once her illness was treated, we were able to help her. I argued that Susan was giving Millie false hope by encouraging her to believe that she'd live on her own someday. But Susan desperately wanted to give Millie hope, and she didn't like to discuss medication with her—understandably so, as it was one of Millie's sore points.

Once when going to the pharmacy, Susan followed her with a camera and asked Millie questions about her medications. Millie immediately became irritated.

"I have to live this way," she snapped. "It makes it twice as unpleasant to talk about it."

This role was always problematic for Susan; she didn't want to be a parent to Millie. In *Out of the Shadow,* she calls it "a crisis of my conscience" and wonders, "Can I be the parent to Millie that she has never been to me?" Of course, Susan did play that role for Millie time and time again, but she had always hoped that Millie could be more independent and had a hard time "policing" her. Millie recognized this reluctance and took advantage of it.

Susan had always been timid around Millie, afraid to assert herself. On the other hand, I engaged Millie directly in various ways. As my sister and I tried to agree on a living situation that was tenable for our mother, we carried those childhood dynamics with us.

Through all of this, I became an enemy of everyone around me—especially Susan—who felt that if Millie didn't want to take medication, why should she? On this topic, Susan and I disagreed vehemently.

I once lied to Millie so she would accept treatment with the necessary medication. Susan felt that lying to her was wrong, no matter the circumstances. Of course, lying to my mother wasn't easy for me. In order to get Millie to sign the consent form required for treatment, I told her it was for something she wanted: the lease to a new apartment. Susan worried what would happen when Millie found out about the deception. Her concerns were warranted. When Millie discovered she hadn't in fact signed the lease to a new apartment, she became enraged.

"What happened to the apartment you promised me, Susan?"

she demanded, sitting on her bed in the psychiatric floor at Good Samaritan Hospital. Susan had no explanation.

"You're just nasty meanies," Millie said.

Susan explained that a bed in a nursing home had opened up, but Mille told her, in no uncertain terms, that she didn't need nursing.

"I'm perfectly healthy. I walk everywhere. I don't drink or smoke or take drugs. I eat properly. I've had it with the United States and my being a fruit lady and you being enema bags."

Millie's rage was understandable. At fifty-nine, she had no home and no one but her daughter—one lying to her and the other filming her suffering—to care for her. We were doing the best we could to get her placed somewhere that would make her happier and less dependent, in an environment where she felt at home and not so helpless.

At the nursing home, Millie was assigned a psychiatrist who had little knowledge of her history and was clearly overworked. Susan and I were back in the position of being responsible for our mother but uninformed about her care.

Finally, we learned that we could have more control over Millie's care if we sued the state of Illinois for guardianship. We filed and won on the basis of Millie's acceptance of our plea and the Guardian for Disabled Adults probate act.

"I won't feel like I'm an orphan anymore," Millie said to us afterward.

During her interview with the lawyer, Millie said that guardianship should have been sought earlier. She said she was happy that her children would be her guardians, that we were good to her, that we were actually "more like sisters" to her.

Millie later told Susan and me that, without guardianship, "I'm always getting kidnapped. Paramedics and police are always kidnapping me. I consider it kidnapping; the whole thing. I'm homesick."

After obtaining guardianship, we were able to get Millie on the waiting list for a group home in DuPage County. The group home atmosphere was exactly what we wanted for Millie, as it would provide structure, stability, social outlets, job training, supervised administration of medications and, most importantly, a place to call home. All we had to do was to wait for an opening at the home.

However, during the interview process, Millie began showing the signs (at least to us) of impending psychosis. Upon looking further into the matter, we discovered that a treating doctor at the nursing home had taken Millie off her antipsychotic medication, Mellaril (which had been withdrawn from the market for safety reasons), but had failed to replace it with another drug.

Susan and I were furious. Our contact at the group home began to question whether Millie was ready for this move. We wrote a letter informing the doctor of the consequences of his actions:

> *On behalf of my sister, Susan Smiley, and I, we are writing to express our disbelief and anger at your neglectful treatment of our mother, Mildred Smiley. As you know, Mildred has been under your care at West Chicago Terrace for close to a year while awaiting placement in a group home.*
>
> *Before Mildred was even placed in West Chicago Terrace, both my sister and I made it clear to the nurses and to you that we are her legal guardians and we need to be informed of any changes whatsoever, whether it be changes in her behavior that require immediate hospitalization and/or changes in her drug therapy. Enclosed in this letter is your second copy of our guardianship papers for Mildred Smiley.*
>
> *In order for Mildred to receive adequate care, Susan and I need to be informed of all possible changes in her drug therapy. We have taken care of our mother for over two decades and we both know the changes that can occur with her when she refuses to take her much-needed antipsychotic medication or, worse yet, is flatly denied them. Also, with as many past hospitalizations and near homelessness situations she has been in, having needed input from caring and concerned family*

members has always been well received and appreciated by the medical staff that has treated her in the past.

As you know, Mildred had a two-month notice for her upcoming health assessment with the DuPage County Health Department for placement in a group home. She was doing quite well and excited about her possible move in the near future. She was stabilized on Mellaril, an antipsychotic and Desyrel, an antidepressant.

But as recently as three weeks ago, she was taken off of her needed antipsychotic medication without our consent. We had no knowledge of the changes in her drug therapy, and when it came time for her health assessment, she was noticeably paranoid and agitated by the questions put to her by the doctors who would recommend placement in the group living environment.

We are aware that Mellaril has been proven to cause heart problems in some patients and that may have been your reasoning for discontinuing that drug, but the fact that you did not replace it with another antipsychotic medication is negligent on your part. If you had informed us of this change we would have insisted that you replace it with another antipsychotic medication.

Because Millie was not taking an antipsychotic at the time of her health assessment, we were concerned that her eligibility for the group home—that would be so beneficial—might be jeopardized.

We hold you solely responsible if she is rejected in the group living environment and we encourage you to speak with the DuPage County Health Department on her behalf as to her benefits to be placed in such a living arrangement and to clarify to them your mishandling of our mother's treatment.

If there are any changes in her medical therapy or treatment, we expect to be notified immediately.

Fortunately, the staff at the group home had seen footage of Susan's film and had a great deal of sympathy for Millie's situation. Her placement was held, and we soon moved her into the group home. Susan and I were delighted and relieved.

The home had been purchased and was owned by the local National Alliance for the Mentally Ill (NAMI) chapter. David Rose, chairman of NAMI's DuPage Housing Committee, explained to Susan and me that the home was leased to the county health department, which provided the staff and funding for services. The Illinois State Department of Public Aid provided funding for eight residents per year at a cost of $35,000 each.

The group home would not have been possible had NAMI not gone to court alleging a violation of federal fair-housing laws in Naperville, Illinois, where a similar group home had faced opposition from a neighboring community. The case had resulted in a landmark ruling.

In a letter to Susan explaining the situation, David Rose also wrote, "Should you ever be moved to produce a sequel to your superb documentary, you might want to consider documenting the great need for community housing for the many mentally ill still locked into living in nursing homes, or on the streets, in spite of federal legislation that dictates that the mentally ill should live in the community to the extent that they are able."

I was in constant communication with the staff at the group home. Early into my mother's stay there, before her new antipsychotic medication could take full effect, Millie had been walking the street in front of the home, talking loudly—and in the aftermath of the Naperville lawsuit, it was important to keep the residents of the group home as inconspicuous as possible. So she was hospitalized for five days until she was stabilized on her new medication.

As a resident of the group home, Millie had the support of a full staff of psychiatrists provided by DuPage County Health Department. Each month, staff from the group home brought Millie to their offices for "med checks" and to make sure her side effects were being managed.

Within a couple of months, Millie began showing signs of great improvement. She was soon employed at Panera Bread as a dishwasher; she loved going to work each day. Millie looked forward to interacting with healthy people, having responsibilities, socializing with friendly coworkers, and earning some money.

Of course, she still fought her medication at times, but she began to understand that among the consequences of noncompliance was losing her job. However, during this time, many of the drugs she was taking began interacting. To treat her side effects the doctors prescribed more medicine, believing that her side effects were symptoms of being undermedicated.

"I'm too much of a purist to be mixed up in all this," Millie told Susan, referring to all her medications. "You're better off going to health food stores. An ounce of prevention is a pound of cure. You're better off not getting sick. Living healthy, staying healthy all your life. Living a full life and avoiding these pitfalls."

In the early 1990s, Susan moved to Los Angeles. Millie would sometimes visit and, when she did, she would sometimes try curtailing or eliminating her medication.

Before Millie's visits, Susan and I talked extensively. Susan felt insulted by my repeated reminders that Millie had to take a dose of her medication the minute she walked in the door and that Susan needed to keep the pills in her possession. But I knew Millie's tricks.

One time, Jeff's sister took Millie to the airport. When they got there, Millie had (supposedly) forgotten her medication. They returned to the group home to get the meds. Although Millie did make her flight, she had become quite anxious. Then, at some point between retrieving her medicine and meeting up with Susan in L.A., Millie took the powder out of her antipsychotic capsules, put the capsules back together, and returned the capsules to the bottle.

So, although Susan did watch Millie take her pills and had a conversation with her each time afterward (to make sure Millie wasn't "cheeking" anything), she failed to check the pills themselves.

The first Sunday after returning from California, Millie was supposed to meet with her cousin Nancy for church and lunch. Nancy picked her up at the group home and, while they were driving, asked Millie where she felt like going to eat.

Millie replied, "I don't want to go to church with you anymore."

Something about Millie's tone suggested to Nancy that she wasn't well. Nancy had been picking Millie up every Sunday for nearly two years, taking her to church and out to lunch. Frightened, Nancy promptly took Millie back to the group home. She didn't call me or Susan. I had spoken with Millie earlier that day, and she had managed to be friendly and talk about the nice time she had visiting Susan. Had I gotten a call from Nancy, though, I would have known right away that Millie was in danger—that she had gone off her antipsychotic.

A week later, I got a call from the group home; Millie had said she wasn't taking her medication anymore and that she was quitting her job at Panera. She admitted to emptying the pills during her trip to see Susan and requested that her psychiatrist lower the dosages of her other medications. She started expressing hatred for everyone and everything, including "the state of Illinois."

Typically, when Millie is not compliant, it takes about two weeks to see the signs of her deterioration. In her mind, she's doing well, and this justifies her noncompliance. After all, a life free of medication is what she wants most. Also, schizophrenia is cyclical; like with some other illnesses, patients experience periods of remission. So while Millie can do well for a time without medication, she can't keep it up for long.

The group home did have a policy of making sure the patients swallowed their medication, but Millie would sometimes hide pills between her bridgework and gum. Not everyone on the staff was aware of how clever she could be.

Though I did wait to see whether the staff would be able to get Millie to comply again and was encouraged by Susan to let them take care of her, my instinct told me I should go see her. I wanted to avert a crisis; every time Millie had a breakdown, she was escorted by police or strapped to a gurney and brought to the psych unit of a hospital.

Late that Sunday, I got another call from the group home: Millie was threatening to kill herself along with everyone around her. It was time to go to her. I took Charles, then almost sixteen, with me. I called Millie and told her I was coming and to hang in there.

Charles and I drove most of the night, then picked up Millie to take her to breakfast and get a feel for how she was doing. As soon as she got in the car, she said, "You don't mind if I don't take a shower for a few days." At breakfast, she started in on her psychiatrist. "If he doesn't die," she said, "I'm going to take a gun to his head." We quickly finished our meal and spent the rest of the morning driving around as I spoke on the phone with her psychiatrist, who was trying to find a hospital bed for Millie.

While I waited for the doctor to call me back with instructions on which hospital to take her to, Millie explained earnestly to Charles about wanting to live on her own and be free. Charles talked to her about his dance classes and his trip abroad.

When the doctor called, we were just one block from the hospital with an available bed.

As soon as Millie realized where we were going, she said, "We're not going to the hospital. I'm not going inside."

I parked the car, got out, and opened the door for Millie. She threatened to disown me. Eventually, though, I was able to persuade her to leave the car. On a bench outside the hospital, people were smoking, and Millie stopped, wanting to smoke with them.

"Those are my kind of people," she said. "They are beautiful people. The people in the hospital are ugly."

When a nurse approached us, I let Charles talk with Millie while I took the nurse aside and explained the situation, showing her a copy of the legal guardianship letter. I told her that my mother had paranoid schizophrenia and that she had recently been noncompliant, leaving her feeling terrified. I alerted the nurse that Millie could seem quite scary and might say things she didn't mean, so it would probably be best to direct questions to me rather than her.

This strategy worked well; while Millie told the nurse how ugly she was, I was able to get her into a hospital gown. I warned her that the doctor was about to come in and that the sooner she complied, the sooner she could return home. Otherwise, she'd just have to stay in the hospital. She listened, not liking the idea of a long hospital stay, and allowed the doctor to give her an injection of an antipsychotic.

Eventually, I had to go home to Minnesota—about five hundred miles from where we were in Elmhurst, Illinois—and Millie was to stay on the psych ward until she was stabilized. Through all of that, I felt grateful to have the opportunity to be with Millie, to be someone she could trust—even though she told me she wished I would keep my distance and called me "horrible" for meddling in her affairs. But separating my emotions from my mother's and realizing it was her illness speaking enabled me to help her—and myself. The group home had made a huge difference in Millie's life, but it had its limitations. They had fought to establish the home in the community, and the last thing I wanted was to have Millie carried away on a stretcher, yelling profanities.

When I left the hospital that day, mustering the trust to leave my mother in the hands of the medical staff, I was exhausted. A sadness swept over me that I had to suppress in front of her. I had to remind myself that when she took her medication, she was capable of having a good life. She'd never be able to live on her own, but the group home, her friends, and her job were the next best thing for Millie.

Before we drove out of the city that night, Charles and I ate at the Panera where Millie worked. I complimented him on how well he had handled things with his grandmother and how important it was to remind her that we loved her and that she was safe. Charles understood that when she behaved as she had that day, it was because she was sick; her medications enabled her to be the grandmother he preferred to be around.

I spoke with the manager of Panera. Although I didn't divulge Millie's illness, I said that Millie had a preexisting medical condition and that she had been suffering some side effects of her medication. I told him Millie would really like to return to work when she was feeling better. The manager was very understanding, saying that they missed her at the restaurant. He went on to tell me that it was hard to find workers like Millie; she was always friendly and upbeat, she came to work on time every day, and she worked very well with the other employees. I nearly broke down in tears.

But the following weekend, I was back again, this time with Jeff. Millie wasn't complying. She was still in the hospital, and the doctor hadn't been returning my calls. A social worker did call requesting Millie's medical history, and when I asked where the doctor was, the social worker informed me that the doctor had left the country a few days prior. Millie had been assigned a new psychiatrist. A week had passed—a week without any antipsychotic medication.

Millie has been in and out of the state mental health system for twenty-five years. As her daughter and her guardian, I know her history inside and out. I know what works and what doesn't. When she's assigned a new doctor who has different ideas about how to treat her, she suffers as a result, especially when the doctor fails to take her history into account.

During a conference with us, Millie's new psychiatrist promised Jeff and me that he would try to give Millie an injection of a new timed-release antipsychotic, as we had requested, but that she had been refusing all medications. He agreed that Millie was not of sound mind but explained that his hands were tied. By law, he was unable to force any medication on Millie. Even if her guardian insisted, Millie had to sign a consent form. He suggested I talk to Millie and try to persuade her to accept the injection.

It's difficult to get into the mind of a person with schizophrenia. Whenever Millie is psychotic, she believes everyone around her is acting bizarrely. She becomes confused about why someone would want to give her an injection. The hospital, to her, is a "dirty, filthy, crazy" place, and she thinks needles are filled with poison. In order to reason with Millie, I had to appeal to her way of thinking. Jeff was with me, and I explained to her that he was on the staff there and that he had spies. I was able to convince Millie that if she would play the game that these "crazy" people were playing, if she willingly took the shot, then she could get out of the hospital sooner. This scheme seemed to make sense to Millie.

Laws about patients' rights vary from state to state; in Illinois, the patient needs to be of sound mind when signing a consent form. And even if the patient has given consent previously, if he or she refuses the medication at the time of administration, the doctor must abide by the patient's wishes. Guardians in some other states have the right to override patients' wishes and give permission to administer medication as long as the patient is deemed a threat to themselves or others.

In Illinois, acquiring this authority would have required going back to court and getting a medical amendment attached to my guardianship papers stating that I had the authority to allow a doctor to give necessary medication to Millie. The problem was that Millie needed treatment right away. I had to go back to my children and Jeff had to return to work, so before we left, I convinced Millie to sign a consent form that would allow the doctors to treat her with the medication necessary to stabilize her condition.

Millie received the injection but refused to take her mood stabilizer and her oral antipsychotic, which they intended to eventually wean her from. This oral antipsychotic would help her to recover more quickly, with less risk of deterioration.

Jeff and I left later that day. On the way home, I called Millie.

"Mom, you're in the driver's seat," I told her, flatly. "You're in control here. If you take your pills, you can get out of the hospital and go back to the group home and have your job back. If not, the health department is looking for a bed in a nursing home."

The words "nursing home" hit her like a ton of bricks. "Oh," she moaned. "Oh no." After that, she agreed to take her pills.

Millie needed to remain in the hospital until she was stable enough to return to the group home. In two weeks, she would need another injection; if she refused that, we'd be back where we started. Even if I called and spoke with the doctor who'd given it to her the first time, there was still nothing he could do.

For Millie, the end of the line is the nursing home. Laws in nursing homes are different in that prior to entering one, patients will have already signed forms allowing doctors to treat them as necessary; therefore, if she were in such a facility and stopped taking her drugs, the treating physicians could sedate her without her permission.

Fortunately, though, Millie took her second injection, and a staff member from the group home picked up Millie and brought her back from the hospital.

Millie had been away for over a month and was afraid the staff and her friends there would be angry with her. Before Millie's return, the staff held a conference with the other residents to talk about how to handle Millie's return and the importance of giving her some space so she could readjust. Everyone was very understanding, but it took Millie a while to feel at home again. The new psychiatrist assigned to her decided to continue giving her shots for a time, which was easier than trying to get her to take her pills consistently.

I felt fortunate to have been able to help Millie, to have been available to her when she needed me. But I was also angry that I had to intervene repeatedly. As many families of mentally ill people will resoundingly agree, the public mental health system simply falls short. Counties don't keep consistent medical records, nurses are overworked, and physicians have little time to spend with their patients. As a result, staff often over-prescribe medication or become careless about histories.

And for the patients who don't have friends or family advocating for them, keeping track of them, there's little hope. With patients' rights laws the way they are, hospitals don't know what to do with people who are psychotic and refusing medication. Often, these patients are turned back onto the streets. We see them acting bizarrely in public, with no family to claim them.

Chapter Twenty-One

Taking Millie Home

For the past three years, I've called Millie several times a week to make sure she sounded healthy and was taking her medication, and I've listened for any clues that something might be wrong. At first, I inquired as a vigilant guardian. But eventually, I began to trust the staff at the group home more and called just to hear her voice.

There were actually times when we talked like mother and daughter. She'd linger, going into detail about people she met on the bus or accidentally letting the sink overflow at work. She'd get excited when a new item was added to the Panera menu and the employees had a tasting party.

I'd just listen as she talked, laughing quietly to myself at what, in our family, became known as "Millie-isms." For example, she loves to quote Zsa Zsa Gabor: "You always have to look your best. You never know when you might get run over by a truck." Once, when I asked her if she'd been having nightmares, she replied with a deadpan, "No, not really. I did have a dream about the mating habits of elk, though."

And there were those uncomfortable times when I'd have to ask how everything was going at the group home. Was she happy? Was she getting along with the staff and her housemates? Was she waking up on time for work?

I'd try to call on weekends to give Millie something to look forward to after a week of unvarying routine—no skipping a dose, no waking up late for work, no escaping the constant reminder that she was a paranoid schizophrenic.

I'd also call on weekends because the kids were home; they'd take turns telling her about their various activities and interests, fighting for time with her. After they'd all had a chance, I would say goodbye and remind her I was proud of her and how much it meant to me to be able to keep in touch and hear her voice.

"Really?" she'd say, astonished by my interest and pride.

To manage the side effects of Millie's various medications properly, her attending psychiatrist relied on input from the group home staff members, who were responsible for administering her pills and monitoring any behavioral changes. Millie did complain to them often about side effects (particularly restless legs and joint problems), and the doctors would usually respond by prescribing an additional drug. She'd been regularly receiving her timed-release antipsychotic injections. Millie also continued to take an oral antipsychotic, even though the Elmhurst psychiatrist had recommended that the drug be tapered. But the county psychiatrist who was treating Millie at the group home never ordered the change.

Millie was taking an arthritis medication, which, we later discovered, elevated her blood pressure and caused dizziness. She was on a mood stabilizer and an anticholinergic drug (to counteract the side effects of her antipsychotics—mostly involuntary movements and restless legs). However, after Millie started taking a new antidepressant medication, the restless legs returned.

Millie's restless legs made it difficult for her to sleep, so she was given a sleep aid. This medicine caused Millie to have a "hung over" feeling in the morning; she would drink six to eight cups of coffee just to get going. Due to all the caffeine, her blood pressure became elevated and her heart rate accelerated. To counter these effects a beta-blocker was prescribed. This treatment aggravated her symptoms of Raynaud's disease—continually cold hands and feet. On top of all that, Millie was given a powerful antibiotic for sinusitis.

The combination of all of these medications—over twelve different kinds—and her body's decreasing ability to metabolize them, compromised her kidney function, which led to a low blood sodium level. The low level of sodium brought on acute short-term memory loss.

Late one night, Jeff and I got a call from the group home. Millie's psychiatrist—the one treating her at the group home—was out of the country for a month, her family physician was unreachable, and the staff needed a physician's opinion. Without examining Millie, it was difficult for Jeff to determine if she was acutely psychotic, so he advised them to withhold her sleeping pills and stop her antibiotic. He felt she might be experiencing side effects from drug interactions. He suggested that she be evaluated in the morning to determine whether she was improving.

The next morning, the staff noticed that Millie was, in fact, feeling better. She had even come downstairs dressed for work, saying she felt fine. That morning, before she left for work, she was given her routine pills, along with her vitamins.

In the meantime, Susan and I had an argument. She wanted to fly to Chicago for the epilogue of *Out of the Shadow*; but I said Millie was not feeling well and shouldn't be filmed. Susan went anyway and did manage to get some footage but admitted that Millie looked terrible; she was pale and confused, walked slowly, and had a fever and chills. I was upset about the filming. I knew that Millie had gotten out of bed that day only to please Susan.

Susan was able to stay in Chicago for only a few days. Three days after she left, Millie went to work but never returned. The other residents of the group home noticed her absence when someone went looking for Millie to set the dinner table. When a staff member called Panera, the manager found Millie sitting outside. She'd been waiting there for two hours, thinking Susan was going to give her a ride back.

The next morning, I got another call from the group home: They'd brought Millie to a crisis center to have a nurse look at her. The nurse immediately called an ambulance, and Millie was taken to Elmhurst Hospital. I packed my bags and was out of the house within half an hour. I didn't have time to find a babysitter, so I brought my seven-year-old daughter Breigha with me.

The staff at Elmhurst had seen *Out of the Shadow*. They had all of Millie's records on file, and my contacts at the hospital were people who knew something about her. I called them, and they told me that they were expecting Millie shortly. Staff from the group home sat with Millie for six hours in the emergency room (ER), insisting something wasn't right with her. And while the nurses in the ER kept trying to get a urine sample from Millie, thinking she could have a urinary tract infection, they discovered that Millie was actually dehydrated. Because she'd been feeling so sick, she'd stopped eating and drinking two days before.

But before I got there, Millie had been seen by the ER physician, who diagnosed her with acute psychosis and sent her to the psych ward. When I called again and found this out on my way there, I phoned the psychiatrist assigned to her care. I explained that, based on my experience, Millie needed immediate medical attention, not a place on the floor. He said she was sound medically, even though she was exhibiting symptoms indicative of TIA's (mini-strokes).

When I hung up, Susan phoned to let me know a nurse from the psych floor had called asking for permission to increase all of Millie's medications; the physicians also wanted to add Haldol. I flipped out.

"They want to give her a chemical lobotomy," I told Susan. "She'll be dead before I get there."

Susan refused their request. I called the floor and told the nurse who'd spoken with Susan not to give her any more drugs. I said I'd be there in about five hours and that, if I had to, I'd carry my mother out of the hospital myself.

I arrived at two that morning, checked into my hotel, napped for an hour, and called Jeff to get a medical opinion so I'd be ready for whatever was thrown at me.

On my way to the hospital, I stopped at the group home to discuss with the staff what they felt had happened with Millie at the ER. By 7:30 a.m., I was on the psych floor, waiting outside the locked doors. I rang the doorbell but was told I had to wait. The staff happened to be, at that moment, in conference regarding Millie. The internist, the social worker supervisor, Millie's assigned psychiatrist, and a nurse from the floor were at the meeting.

Afterward, as the internist was telling me that Millie wasn't awake yet, my mother shuffled into the room, as if she'd sensed that I had come. She could barely walk. She appeared to have lost ten pounds, her features were pale and gaunt, and the skin on her lips was peeling. She looked like a walking skeleton.

She began telling me about a sweater of hers that looked like the one my daughter was wearing that day. Then she started talking about people and places I'd never heard of, things I couldn't understand. Her voice was barely audible. I thought, *My mother is dying before my eyes, and they have her locked up in a psych ward.*

Seeing my mother reduced to a zombie made me want to cry out to her. But she was frightened herself—I could see it in her eyes. I swallowed hard, reminding myself I was not only her daughter but also her advocate: I needed to be strong for her.

I turned to the internist. "This woman is very sick," I told him firmly and calmly. "She needs immediate medical attention."

He replied that he already had a bed available for her.

All of Millie's medication was stopped for two days. She had an elevated white blood cell count, and they needed to determine what was causing that. They performed a chest X-ray and found some cloudiness in one of her lungs, so she was treated with two broad-spectrum antibiotics. By this time, she was having stroke-like symptoms—one minute, she could talk and make sense, the next she was disoriented. I insisted that a neurologist see her immediately, but it often takes up to forty-eight hours for a neurologist's in-person examination. After she was transferred, the nurse suggested that I watch her breathing to be sure she wasn't having a stroke. As far as I could tell, Millie was unconscious.

When the neurologist finally arrived later that day, Millie was incoherent. He seemed irritated by my demand that he come immediately. He ordered an MRI and, although there was no evidence of a stroke, other tests showed that Millie had developed pneumonia, dehydration, the start of kidney failure, and sepsis (a condition caused by the presence of toxins in the blood).

I asked the internist to order a chemical toxicity test to determine whether Millie's symptoms were chemically induced, but he refused.

Millie said to me weakly, "I'm too small to be on so many drugs." Later, once she was feeling better, Millie told me, "They don't know what they're doing. They [mentally ill] just get worse all the time. They don't know what they're doing with the drugs. There's no way of testing someone's brain, put a needle in it and take out the chemicals. Psychiatric problems in the United States just keep getting worse and worse and worse. And hanging around with sick people, I can just get sick myself . . . from them."

Once Millie's condition was stabilized, my daughter and I returned to our hotel. Exhausted, I phoned Susan and asked her to check in with the nurses from time to time. Susan agreed to call every hour. Yet, later that night, I got a call from the floor nurse, asking me to okay a mood stabilizer for Millie.

"Absolutely not," I snapped. "What part of Millie's med sheet didn't you understand? We're weaning her off. Can't you see that?"

The nurse explained that Millie had been having trouble sleeping; she wanted to avoid "problems" on the ward.

"When these patients complain," she added, "they can get a little loud."

I hung up the receiver.

Five minutes later, the telephone rang again. The group home said the same nurse had just called, trying to get someone there to okay the mood stabilizer. They told me the nurse had said she didn't want Millie to "lose it on her."

When I called the nurse back, I said, "I could make it easier on you and write 'psych' on her forehead."

Afterward, I sat for a moment, head spinning. Then, I called Jeff. We'd discussed the possibility for years. I told him that it was time. I wanted to take my mother home.

The next morning, I went to see Millie at the hospital but waited to talk to her about my decision. I wanted her to be stabilized first. She'd slept well the night before, without the sleeping pill, and without the mood stabilizer. She seemed to be feeling better, even though she was a little groggy and tired from the ordeal of the past few days.

I told her I'd be back later and took Breigha to lunch. Susan called to let me know that Alan had just gotten home from the hospital—he'd been rushed to the ER for complications due to an enlarged prostate. I called Nancy to tell her what was happening with Millie, that I was in town, and that I'd come to see my father.

When I arrived, Alan seemed slow and weak but otherwise okay. We chatted pleasantly for a bit, and he had a chance to catch up with Breigha, whom he hadn't seen in several months. Then, unexpectedly, he began to cry.

"It's not that I didn't love your mother," he said, as if it had been the first thing on his mind. "I did. I just didn't understand her."

My father had caught me totally by surprise; for a moment, I did not know what to say.

"Why are you regretting this now?" I asked him.

"I regret leaving you kids behind," he said to me. "I couldn't fight it."

For the first time, looking at my father, I realized how frightened he was. Perhaps, when he'd been lying in that hospital bed, he was afraid that he might die.

I asked myself, *Can I love this man after everything that's happened?*

He continued to talk about long-ago events as if they had all just happened yesterday—how my uncle wouldn't let him in the door the night I'd attempted suicide, how he'd left Millie but tried to put her in a position to get support from Kathryn, how Millie's stepbrother Wes played hardball with him when he'd tried to gain custody of me.

"Dad," I said, finally. "None of that matters now."

I explained to him how close Millie had come to dying and that I no longer had the strength to shuttle back and forth between Minnesota and Illinois. I told him that I was taking my mother home with me.

He was concerned, but I assured him.

"Don't regret this," I said, "You have what you always wanted, and I have a beautiful family."

That Saturday, Millie was discharged. She was thrilled to be going home with us. When I called the house, Eddie, then thirteen, answered.

"One of my dreams came true, Mom," he said.

"What's that?" I asked him.

"Grandma Millie's gonna live with us." Then he added, "My other dream is to get into the NBA."

I had never been so happy to leave a hospital in my life, and I don't think Millie had, either. We went to the group home, packed up Millie's things, and said our good-byes. One of the staff members took me aside and said the whole experience with Millie had really opened her eyes. She had no idea how bad things were.

Then Millie, Breigha, and I headed north. Before we reached the state line, Millie left a message for Susan.

"I'm leaving," she said with a lilt in her voice I hadn't heard in years. "No more Illinois."

Millie picking blueberries with her granddaughter in Minnesota. 2003

Postscript

Naming an illness can suddenly define someone's identity—a cancer victim, a heart patient, an epileptic, a cancer survivor.

In the mental health community, people diagnosed with schizophrenia are often said to be "suffering from schizophrenia," but rarely is there any reference to survival, to the language of hope. Millie, then, became a schizophrenic—a *sufferer* of schizophrenia for which there is no cure, only treatment—and this meant that the relief we felt in solving the riddle of our lives inevitably gave way to the long and difficult road ahead of us.

The American Psychiatric Association's *Diagnostic and Statistical Manual for Mental Disorders (DSM)* has classified five types of schizophrenia: disorganized, catatonic, paranoid, residual, and undifferentiated. *DSM-IV-TR*, the most recent revision, continues to employ these classifications, though it's commonly understood that they aren't accurate in predicting the outcome of the illness. Rather, they provide mental health professionals with a structure and system for diagnosis and treatment. With schizophrenia, no two sufferers are alike. Symptoms vary widely, and treatments, as for most mental illnesses, rely largely on trial and error. That's one reason why treating schizophrenia is so challenging. It can take years to find a combination of medications that will work for an individual.

Every time a person suffers a psychotic episode, there's an increase in brain damage, and episodes often worsen with time. Millie had likely suffered countless episodes by the time she was diagnosed. She lived without appropriate treatment for twenty years. I mourn all those lost years of her life.

I've wanted so much to reach out to this woman, my mother, who has rarely had an easy day in her life, a day free of paranoia, medication, depression, and fear.

With the exception of raising three children, being my mother's legal guardian is the most challenging aspect of my life. I often have been resentful, tired, overwhelmed, angry, and frustrated. I lived—sometimes for weeks—in fear that the telephone would ring in the middle of the night. Some days, I would have given anything to be free of this responsibility.

Over the years, I've gotten many compliments from mental health providers dealing with Millie. They've said to me, essentially, that if I hadn't gotten involved in my mother's care, she wouldn't be doing as well as she is. And I think of all the other families out there who are so exasperated that they are forced to abandon their family members.

Sometimes, I find myself wondering why, if schizophrenia affects one in every hundred people, we were given this particular challenge in our lives. And I think of all that Millie has gone through. Her cousin Nancy once asked her, "When have things ever felt right for you?" Millie replied, "I've never been right. Nothing has ever been right for me."

Now, Millie is home with my family. Though, of course, that raises different issues.

Trying to accommodate Millie without resenting her because of her needs and without treating her as if she's helpless while also meeting all the other demands in our lives hasn't been easy. My husband, my children, and I have had to find ways to adjust our lives to let her in as well as respect her space; we've also had to be firm with her, at times, about respecting ours.

My mother requires a lot of attention; she is currently unemployed, though she does have chores around the house. Her memory and ability to task are impaired and she needs frequent reminders to take her medications. She is asked by her grandchildren to play board games, such as "Monopoly," but she often forgets where her playing chip is on the board.

Before Millie moved in with us, I had a counselor for the local human services department come over to help me educate my children about schizophrenia—after all, they witness Millie taking her medications daily. Often, they have a better understanding of their grandmother than I give them credit for.

But, above all, I hope the experience of living with their grandmother instills in my children the idea that running from a complicated situation won't solve anything.

For them, one of the most difficult aspects of Millie's illness to understand—and one of the most baffling characteristics of schizophrenia itself—is the general lack of insight. In *Out of the Shadow,* Millie is shown being asked if she understands paranoid schizophrenia.

"I never understood that. I understand paranoia, yes, but schizophrenia, no."

When Susan decided to film *Out of the Shadow,* she did so out of frustration. She was hoping to show what one person afflicted with schizophrenia went through in a fractured system. She'd had a good deal of experience producing documentary films, from working on *Dangerous Missions*—which told stories of the most dangerous jobs in the United States—to traveling to Alaska to shoot *Ice Road Truckers* and to Bosnia to produce a film about dismantling land mines. She'd gone down some rough roads and shot some challenging topics. *Out of the Shadow,* I believe, was one of her toughest projects.

When she first mentioned to me that she wanted to start bringing her camera with her every time we whisked into Chicago to save Millie from peril, I thought it was a great idea. I admired Susan for her talent and her willingness to use film to speak for the Millies of our world. But it didn't occur to either of us, then, that her project would take us back to a time and place we would have much rather kept hidden.

While Susan was interviewing me one night for the film, I brought up the abuse. We had never spoken about the years we were abused by Millie, and I thought it was time we broke the silence. Susan bit her lip and told me she didn't want to talk about it; in the film, she admits that she "didn't want to go there."

I told her, "If you're going to do a film about this, you need to show all of it."

Susan left that night, unwilling to discuss it. And I got mononucleosis and pneumonia, which I attributed to the anguish and the tension of finally speaking about the unspeakable.

Susan took some time to think things over and came back to Minnesota to continue our interview. This time, she asked about my suicide attempt. Waves of emotions coursed through me as I spoke. No one, aside from my immediate family, had ever heard about that time in my life. I'd never before told my story.

For the first time, we talked about the night Susan moved out. She said she thought I would be okay because it appeared that my relationship with Millie was strong, that I knew how to calm her. Susan confessed that she thought I had hated her, and I admitted that I thought I had been the cause of her beatings. And, for the first time in many years, Susan and I cried together. She held my hand and swore to me she would never do anything to hurt me. It wasn't until that night that I realized Susan had left in order to survive.

When the interview ended, after we'd been able to tell our stories together, we began to heal, individually and together. We realized, through this experience, how much we had needed each other all those years and how much Millie needed us still. To this day, Susan and I have disagreements—we have our blow-ups and awkward periods of silence—but we've come farther together than I ever believed we could. And when I think about Millie and how many sacrifices Susan and I have made to save her, I wonder what happens to mentally ill people who don't have advocates like Susan and me. And naturally, I wonder about those advocates who don't have someone else to lean on when things get tough—who don't, at the very least, have each other.

Each year as many as 225,000 people die in the United States from adverse medical reactions. Our current system works by putting out fires, not preventing them. The very laws enacted to protect the rights of patients nearly prevented Millie from getting proper treatment and almost caused her death. Our voices were not heard, and when Millie was ill, she didn't have a voice. Instead, she said, her illness was "rammed down her throat." She said that no matter where she went in the system, she could never get away from the label she had been given.

Millie knew she was being poisoned. But after a while, she said, she just gave up. She calls the people who gave her the medicine the "do-gooders": They meant to help and had no idea that they were causing harm instead.

The state-funded facilities that Millie went to for treatment all had the same feel—sterile and cold, with stark white walls and mass-produced artwork. It began to feel to Millie as if she was intentionally separated from society, that she was an outcast—hardly conducive to healing or wellness.

Now after a year since Millie moved in with us, I'd like to say she is doing better. But knowing that she may have permanent impaired cognitive abilities, what has transpired is nothing less than a miracle. The medications she had been prescribed while in Illinois was replaced by a comprehensive medical program utilizing orthomolecular medicine, often not an option for people with mental illnesses in this country.

Orthomolecular medicine and the treatment of mental illness, in particular schizophrenia, *aims to restore the optimum environment of the body by correcting imbalances or deficiencies based on individual biochemistry using substances natural to the body, such as vitamins, minerals, amino acids, trace elements, and essential fatty acids.*[1]

With the guidance of my husband, an Osteopathic family physician and the unfailing encouragement of her family, and help from an award-winning home health care program, Millie is regaining her strength, her zest for life, and has been able to become independent.

No matter how well she's doing, or how much her health improves, Millie will always have paranoid schizophrenia. Her illness will never go away. She knows this.

"Being called paranoid schizophrenic is more important, even, than what my name is . . . Mildred Smiley. It hurts, yes."

But for the first time in her life, Millie feels safe. And we're hoping that in the company of those who love her, in a place she can call home, she just might flourish after all.

---

[1] http://orthomed.com

For additional Associations, Websites and Recommended Reading, log onto www.extraordinaryvoices.com

Call to Action

Mental Health: A Report of the Surgeon General devotes an entire chapter to outlining a vision for the future of mental health care in the United States. While the *Report* identifies eight initiatives toward the realization of this vision, I wish to focus on the one I consider most fundamental and essential—prevention.

The *Report*, first and foremost, states that the national health care system should base its work on the best available science, thereby preventing disease and promoting good mental and physical health. Therefore, mental health research, especially in the areas of illness prevention and good mental hygiene, is critical to the overall plan for improvement.

Within this vital area of prevention, children who grow up surrounded by complex adult issues such as divorce, drug abuse, mental illness, and emotional and physical trauma often slowly lose their sense of identity and their very childhood, referred to as *ambiguous loss*. Behind a mask of confidence and self-reliance lie feelings of uncertainty, sadness, and loss; these children know, on some level, that they have missed something, yet don't comprehend the loss of childhood and the feelings it raises as a result.

This trauma, experienced by so many children in this country and throughout the world, has all too often gone unrecognized or ignored by health care providers. The lack of knowledge, understanding, and common experiences among these children has left a void of ignorance and misdiagnosis within the medical system, especially in regard to mental and emotional illnesses.

One cannot have good overall health and well-being without good mental health; the ability to thrive in life depends upon it. Yet growing up isolated from the knowledge that we are not alone, that experiences in childhood can lead to an erroneous belief that there is something wrong, that pieces of childhood were lost, many of us, as adult children, become part of the health care system that keeps our identity invisible. Alone, we have no idea that we remain isolated and, consequently, misdiagnosed.

In an attempt to respond, schools screen students for depression beginning in preschool, offering referrals to providers who often medicate these children at a very young age. Also, districts across the country have turned to daily all-day kindergarten, insisting this saves taxpayer money and better educates children.

But the cost of providing health care to families with children who need medications or counseling has risen exponentially in recent years. The health care system has become overburdened with delivering services to people who want quick fixes for colds, flu, viruses, and even mental illnesses. Emergency rooms have become outpatient care centers. Hospital wards are full, treating great numbers of patients with heart disease, diabetes, and other major health problems that, in some cases, have been brought on by poor mental health.

Despite the good intentions of the medical system that treats these diseases, one area that remains invisible is that of complementary family involvement. Many advocates for the mentally ill are family members or close friends. Yet all too often families have felt forced to abandon their own family members, because the stress of finding support for themselves, keeping their own lives in check without support, has become so burdensome that they see no other choice. What good are we to others if we cannot care for ourselves?

There have been many times when I wondered whether I had the mental and physical stamina to deal with Millie's illness, the patience to deal with my teenage son's rebellious nature, or the time to finish this book. Every time I wondered if I had the strength, I reminded myself that if I did not write the story, if I did not document these struggles, both I and the many thousands of other Daughters and Sons would remain as we have always been: invisible.

My goal with the publication of this manuscript is the expansion and strengthening of existing, award-winning programs within the health care delivery system. A few of these programs, which I have listed on the resource page, offer real solutions for prevention, and answers to problems that exist within our society.

Medicine must look within its own structure and facilitate a complementary solution to health care needs that allows for us—family members, neighbors, friends—to ease the load on the over-burdened health care system that cannot provide us with a quick fix.

We must realize that there are no quick-and-easy answers to the current mental health crisis in the U.S. But we can find solutions that will make a difference in the way we treat our neighbors and ourselves. We must learn to find comfort despite our experiences. We must, as Daughters and Sons unite and become *Extraordinary Voices* so we can not only make a difference with the way we are treated, but make a change that we all can be proud of. We must simply find the will to do so.

When Your Parent Has a Mental Illness

Growing up in any family can be challenging at times, but there are often special problems and challenges for families in which one or both parents have a mental illness. Children in these families often have to deal with instability or unpredictability. Often there is confusion in family roles and children have to take over many of the adult responsibilities, such as taking care of younger brothers and sisters or managing household duties normally managed by adults. They may even have the responsibility of taking care of the emotional or physical needs of their parents.

Children in these situations do not always receive the parental care and nurturing they need. Often they feel ashamed to talk about their situation with others and consequently may withdraw from relatives or friends who could help them or support them. Often unable to articulate their needs, even to themselves, these children frequently feel isolated and alone.

Children of mentally ill parents may also experience added difficulties as adults. These may include:

Relationship difficulties:

- difficulty in initiating relationships, and experiencing feelings of isolation
- difficulty in romantic relationships
- difficulty in maintaining friendships
- difficulty with trusting self and others
- difficulty balancing level of intimacy (excessive dependence or excessive avoidance)
- difficulty balancing taking care of self and taking care of others

Emotional difficulties:

- guilt, resentment
- shame, embarrassment
- depression
- fear of inheriting parent's mental illness
- fear of discovery by partner, friends
- inability to express anger constructively, angry outbursts or repressed anger
- confusion about one's own identity
- negative outlook on life
- inability to deal with life unless it is chaotic or in crisis
- overly responsible or irresponsible in many areas of life such as commitments, money, alcohol, relationships, etc.
- self defeating thoughts, attitudes, and behaviors such as "I don't matter; I'm not worth much; It's no use trying."
- self defeating themes involving a tendency to equate achievement with worth as a person, such as: "Maybe I can matter if I can excel at something, be perfect in school, my job, my relationships. But if I fail, I'm worthless and it's terrible."

If you are experiencing any of these difficulties, you are not alone. It is helpful to recognize that these problematic feelings and behaviors helped you to cope and survive the more vulnerable years of childhood. Your recognition that they limit your life choices as an adult is the beginning of your search for more rewarding and functional ways of relating.

How You Can Help Yourself:

1. Acknowledge that you have a parent with a mental illness and acknowledge the effects this has had on you.

- acknowledge previously inadmissible feelings such as anger, shame, guilt, etc.
- grieve the parental support you never received.
- remember that you are not responsible for causing your parent's problems or for fixing his/her condition.

2. Develop new ways of taking care of yourself.

- recognize your own legitimate needs and begin taking care of them
- recognize the stressors in your life, and learn ways of managing them.
- replace negative thoughts with more positive statements: "I am a worthwhile person. This truth does not depend on my successes or failures. My life has ups and downs, but my worth does not change."

3. Develop new ways of relating to others.

- recognize old unhealthy family patterns of communicating, and practice new ways of relating to parents and other family members.
- recognize the difficulties you have with relationships, and learn new ways of relating to others.
- appreciate and enjoy stability in your relationships, recognizing that relationships don't have to be defined by crisis or dependency.

4. Explore other resources.

Educate yourself about your parent's illness.

This can help you understand what your parent is facing and what has caused problems for your family. It can also aid in relieving your feelings of guilt, resentment, embarrassment, and shame.

Consider seeing a mental health professional.

A counselor can help you understand how your parent's illness impacts your life. Also a counselor can help you learn healthier ways of relating to others and caring for your own needs.

Join a support group.

A support group that addresses your specific situation can help reduce feelings of isolation. Seeking such support can be especially helpful when family members are either uncomfortable with or refuse to acknowledge the problem.

Reprinted with permission from the Counseling Center at the University of Illinois, Champaign, Illinois.

Resources

ORGANIZATIONS

National Network of Adult and Adolescent Children Who Have a Mentally Ill Parent
(Australia)
NNAAMI
P.O. Box 213 Glen Iris. 3146
Melbourne, Victoria. Australia
http://home.vicnet.net.au/~nnaami

National Alliance on Mental Health
NAMI
Colonial Place Three
2107 Wilson Blvd., Suite 300
Arlington, VA 22201-3042
1-800-950-NAMI (6264)
www.nami.org

Geriatric Mental Health Foundation
7910 Woodmont Ave, Suite 1050
Bethesda, MD 20814
301.654.7850
www.gmhfonline.org/gmhf

American College for Advancement in Medicine
23121 Verdugo Drive
Suite 204
Laguna Hills, CA 92653
1-800-532-3688
www.acam.org

American Osteopathic Association
Chicago Office – Main Headquarters
142 East Ontario Street
Chicago, IL 60611
Toll-free phone: (800) 621-1773
www.osteopathic.org

National Institute of Mental Health
National Institute of Mental Health (NIMH)
Public Information and Communications Branch
6001 Executive Boulevard, Room 8184, MSC 9663
Bethesda, MD 20892-9663
1-866-615-6464 (toll-free)
www.nimh.nih.gov

National Mental Health Association
2000 N. Beauregard Street, 6th Floor
Alexandria, VA 22311
703/684-7722
www.nmha.org

Canadian Mental Health Association
Canadian Mental Health Association
8 King Street East, Suite 810
Toronto ON M5C 1B5
www.cmha.ca/bins/index.asp

American Psychiatric Association
1000 Wilson Boulevard
Suite 1825
Arlington, VA 22209
www.healthyminds.org

International Society for Orthomolecular Medicine
16 Florence Ave
Toronto, Ontario
Canada M2N 1E9
www.orthomed.org/ISOM/isom.html

For additional Associations log onto:
www.extraordinaryvoices.com

WEB SITES

Campaign for Mental Health Reform
www.mhreform.org

Extraordinary Voices Website and Forum
www.extraordinaryvoices.com
www.extraordinaryvoices.com/cgi/yabb2/YaBB.cgi

For Parents with a Mental Illness
www.parentingwell.com

National Mental Health Association
www.nmha.org

Invisible Children's Project
www.nmha.org/children/invisibleinfo.cfm

National Network of Adult and Adolescent Children Who Have a Mentally Ill Parent/s (Australia)
www.home.vicnet.net.au/~nnaami

National Center for PTSD
www.ncptsd.va.gov/index.html

Bikers Against Child Abuse
www.bacausa.com

Orthomolecular Medicine Online
www.orthomed.org

Mental Health Parity Act of 1996
http://new.cms.hhs.gov/HealthInsReformforConsume/04_TheMentalHealthParityAct.asp

Substance Abuse and Mental Health Services Administration
http://www.samhsa.gov

For additional Resources log onto: www.extraordinaryvoices.com

PROGRAMS

Two award-winning programs that have proven positive results and considerable cost savings to counties that have these programs in place.

Weekend Consequential Camp is a short-term, inexpensive response for kids:

- breaking curfew and other home rules
- being truant or misbehaving at school
- violating probation contracts and case plans

Intended to be a consequence for some misbehavior—a response intended to deter future misbehavior. More importantly, it is an opportunity for kids to reflect on the choices they make.

Information about this pilot program is not available online but can be obtained by writing to:

Gerry Buse –WCC
Watonwan County Human Services
715 2nd Ave S
St. James, MN 56081

Invisible Children's Project (ICP)

Developed to provide integrated essential services to parents with treatment needs to increase their ability to function in their communities and assist them in creating a safe and nurturing environment for their children.

Further information about this program can be found on the resource page at: www.extraordinaryvoices.com

Note:
If you would like your program added to this resource list, please contact the author with the following information:

Name of the program
Project overview
Project information
Project sites
Services
Outcomes
Funding (federally funded or privately funded)

Recommended Reading

Amador, Xavier, with Johanson, Anna-Lisa.
I Am Not Sick, I Don't Need Help! Peconic, NU: Vida, 2000.

Carter, Rosalynn, with Golant, Susan K.
Helping Someone with Mental Illness: A Compassionate Guide for Family, Friends, and Caregivers. New York: Three Rivers, 1999.

Brown, E.M.
My Parent's Keeper; Adult Children of the Emotionally Disturbed, 1989.

Hobson, J. Allan, and Leonard, Jonathan A.
Out of Its Mind: Psychiatry in Crisis. New York: Perseus, 2002.

Hoffer, Abram; Walker, Morton; and Pauling, Linus.
Putting It All Together: The New Orthomolecular Nutrition.
New Canaan, CT: Keats, 1998.

Lesser, Michael, with Kapklein, Colleen.
The Brain Chemistry Diet. New York: Putnam, 2002.

Torrey, E. Fuller.
Out of the Shadows: Confronting America's Mental Illness Crisis.
New York: John Wiley & Sons, 1998.

__________,
Surviving Schizophrenia: A Manual for Families, Consumers, and Providers.
4th ed. New York: HarperCollins, 2001.

Willett, Walter C.
Eat, Drink, and Be Healthy. New York: Simon & Schuster, 2001.